Walking Through Fire

Cobus The Viking Visser

COBUS VISSER

"I am here for a purpose and that purpose is to grow into a mountain, not to shrink to a grain of sand. Henceforth, will I apply ALL my efforts to become the highest mountain of all and I will strain my potential until it cries for mercy."

Og Mandino

The Boy and the Map

One day, a young boy was bored. He asked his mother to play with him. She was busy and told him to go and play with his father. The father, who was also busy, tried to buy some time. He found a Time magazine and came across a picture of a map of the world. He tore the map into strips and squares, shuffled it, and put it in a box.

He said, "Son, go to your room and put the map together. When you're done, we can play."

The father thought that it would take the boy at least an hour to put the map together. About 15 minutes later, the boy called his dad. When his dad entered the room, he showed him that he had put the map together.

The father was astounded and asked, "How did you do it so quickly, son?"

The son answered, "It was easy, Dad. At the back of the map was a picture of a man. I figured that if I got the man right, the world would fall into place."

This story is about getting the man right so that his world can fall into place.

Contents Page

In the realm of extraordinary individuals, there exists an unassuming yet profoundly influential figure whose essence reverberates through the lives he touches. This memoir serves as a testament to the incredible impact and remarkable legacy of a dear friend and special soul, Cobus Visser. He is an individual who has shattered barriers, defied odds, and is a man I am deeply inspired by.

Cobus's life is an anthem of resilience, courage, and unyielding determination. Despite a debilitating illness, Cobus has embraced adversity as a catalyst for change, transcending the limitations imposed by circumstance.

When I first met him, he was in a wheelchair, challenged by his haemophilia and the restrictions it placed on his being. Fast forward 9 years, and I've witnessed him bungy jump off buildings in New Zealand, climb Mount Kilimanjaro, and, most importantly, alter and inspire the lives of thousands around the globe.

His journey is an intricate artwork pieced together with perseverance, empathy, and unwavering faith. Through his trials, which would have shattered most, he gained invaluable lessons, nurturing a never-drying cup of empathy that seeks to serve every soul he encounters.

The essence of his being radiates an infectious zest for life, transcending boundaries of age, culture, race and circumstance. He is not merely a catalyst for change but a living embodiment of the strength of the human spirit.

I am truly honoured and blessed to call him friend, colleague, associate and mentor because I learn so much from Cobus through his way of being. May his work continue to inspire the masses as we navigate through this challenging and exciting time in history. Cobus is a legend, a leader, and a king among men.

ROBIN BANKS

INTERNATIONAL SPEAKER AND MIND POWER COACH

November 19, 2011, was when I first met Cobus Visser during a firewalk event for our Kaizen wealth experience, and I was immediately struck by his unyielding spirit and determination. That day, as we walked on fire and even broke arrows together, I saw in Cobus a reflection of the very essence of what it means to live with purpose and resilience. The quote from Og Mandino, "I am here for a purpose; that purpose is to grow into a mountain, not to shrink to a grain of sand. Henceforth will I apply all my efforts to become the highest mountain of all, and I will strain my potential until it cries for mercy," which I hold dear, resonated deeply with Cobus. So much so that he went and tattooed it on his heart. It became a guiding beacon for him, just as it had been for me.

Cobus has been more than just a student at Wealth Creators University; he has been a top leader, achieving over 10,000% growth in his business—an extraordinary feat that he has the certificate to prove. Through my retreats, books, and trainings, I have seen Cobus transmute obstacles into opportunities and set new benchmarks for success and inspiration.

This memoir is a testament to Cobus's incredible journey. It chronicles not just his physical acts of walking on fire but his metaphorical walk through the fires of life's adversities, emerging stronger and more resolute each time. His story is one of courage, tenacity, and the relentless pursuit of greatness.

Cobus's journey has been an inspiration to me, as I hope my mentorship has been to him. His ability to overcome seemingly insurmountable obstacles and his dedication to helping others do the same exemplify the core principles of wealth creation and personal empowerment that I have dedicated my life to teaching.

In this book, you will find the raw, unfiltered experiences of a man who embodies the spirit of #whateverittakes. Cobus's story is not just about achieving financial success but about the holistic approach to wealth in all its forms—emotional, physical, and spiritual. His life is a living testament to the Formula for Riches™ and the power of a purpose-driven existence.

I am honoured to write the foreword for this remarkable memoir. Cobus, you are not just a testament to the teachings of Wealth Creators University, but a shining example of what can be achieved when one lives with purpose, passion, and perseverance.

To the readers, may this book ignite the fire within you to pursue your dreams with unwavering commitment. May you, like Cobus, walk through your fires and emerge stronger, ready to take on the world.

With great admiration and respect,

Dr. Hannes Dreyer
Wealth Creator, Mentor, Author, and Speaker
Founder of Wealth Creators University

Today I share with you a journey that ultimately transformed me. As the operator of Haines Fleet, a vehicle fleet management company in Ireland, we have weathered financial storms to maintain a 100% credit rating, living by our ethos, "Small enough to care, experienced enough to deliver." With years of business under my belt, nothing could have prepared me for the mental toll of the pandemic.

Covid-19 struck as a global crisis unparalleled since the last World War, testing my mental resilience. In 2020, I sought solace in the power of the mind and discovered Robin Banks, a Mind Power Advocate, whose insights resonated with me. But it was my encounter with Cobus Visser, a colleague of Robin, that would usher in a new chapter of my life. After months of enlightening conversations, Cobus extended an invitation to his firewalking retreat in South Africa that October—an offer I eagerly accepted, hoping to embrace my fears head-on.

The experience was nothing short of revelatory. Arriving in Johannesburg in late September 2021, Cobus had an uncanny ability to unite a diverse group of individuals from across the globe, dissolving any sense of estrangement among us. Contrary to my expectations, the firewalk was not a lengthy initiation but an immediate leap into self-discovery. With each step across the coals, the haze of uncertainty that plagued my thoughts cleared, leaving in its wake an indescribable liberation.

This newfound clarity was not fleeting. I have since repeated the firewalking ritual, most recently in Sweden, with Cobus and an international assembly of forty-nine participants. The experiences have evocatively altered my perspective on fear, ushering in a plethora of enriching relationships and a zest for life I had not known before.

Reflecting on these gatherings, including Cobus's memorable fortieth birthday in November 2022, I can assert that the impact of these events has been nothing short of transformative. Cobus, a figure of inspiration, demonstrates an unmoving tenacity in overcoming any impediments that cross his path. This firewalk experience has not only renewed my spirit but also connected me with a global community that cherishes the power of human fortitude.

In sharing this account, I pay homage to the incredible influence of Cobus Visser, a man who has not only reshaped my understanding of courage but also proved to be a beacon of hope and inspiration for many, myself included.

Letters To My Family

I owe everything to my family, who have supported me through my trials and tribulations. I haven't always gotten it right, but know that I love you.

Dear Mom,

This letter is for you, Mom—my anchor and my guide. As I pen these words, my heart is full of gratitude for the countless sacrifices you've made, the endless gifts, the financial support, and the unshaking love you've showered upon Tiaan, Wihan, and me.

Reflecting on our journey together, I remember the stress you endured during my hospital stays, our frequent visits to the haemophiliac clinic, and the countless times you faced doctors and physiotherapists.

Through it all, you did the best you could with the knowledge and resources at your disposal. For all of this, I owe you an immense debt of gratitude. I know it was a difficult journey for you to look after me, and yet your strength and perseverance never wavered.

Thank you for your prayers and for being there in every way you could—whether it was ensuring I had a roof over my head, food to eat, clothes to wear, or discreetly putting diesel in my car. The money you left under my pillow and the funds you slipped into my hand were lifelines in my moments of need. You may never fully understand how much your love and acts of kindness meant to me during those difficult times.

While growing up, I saw you handle predicaments mostly by yourself, especially when Dad was stationed at the border or away with the police.

Your hardiness in those times taught me so much about being stronger and more determined.

I think I got my caring nature from you. Perhaps, too, your dedication to helping others and your strong faith in God. Your prayers and reminders to keep faith have been a guiding light for me, encouraging me never to give up, no matter the obstacles.

I love you, Mom, and I promise that one day I will make you proud through the impact I hope to have on people around the world. I truly believe I was born to you for a reason—to learn, to grow, and to be prepared to help others.

I appreciate how you have always been there for me. Whether it was flying out to Kilimanjaro when I was in the hospital during my climb or being by my side during every health crisis, you have always been there. And, yes, I forgive you for the accident with my dog when I was younger; I understand it was just that—an accident.

Though we may not have shared many hugs or often said, "I love you," you showed your love through your actions and your gifts. You always believed in me and boosted my confidence by comparing me to our great-grandfather, CR Swart. You've always said that I am smart, capable, and a genius like him.

Thank you for everything, Mom. I am eternally grateful for all that you are and all that you've done. Your belief in me has shaped the person I am today.

Reflecting on my childhood and the man I've become, I see your influence in every part of my life. You were not just my father but also my hero—the police officer, the sportsman, the head boy in school, the grandson of CR Swart. I have always tried to meet the high standards set by your achievements. I constantly hoped to hear you say, "I am proud of you."

Even though you had a demanding career and were often away or busy at the station, the times we spent together are the ones I remember most fondly. Every experience with you—driving to Johannesburg to get furniture or visiting your office— taught me important lessons about life.

Our relationship experienced its most significant period of growth unexpectedly during the Covid-19 lockdown. Our daily walks and heartfelt conversations on the farm helped bring us closer despite the time and misunderstandings. During these walks, I started to grasp the extent of your experiences and the range of your sacrifices.

Joining the business you created was an honour. I learned not only about marketing under your guidance but also about dedication, leadership, innovative thinking, and the courage to take risks. Leaving the business was one of the hardest decisions I've ever made, and I know it disappointed you.

The space it created allowed me to grow independently. I also saw the sacrifices you made for our family, working tirelessly and even sacrificing early retirement for our prosperity.

You taught me to work hard, face difficulties, and gather knowledge for the future so that I have wisdom and experiences to rely on.

Though I was not always the son you might have envisioned, I have strived to embody the best of what you taught me. I know I wasn't perfect, and perhaps I still have a long way to go to truly make you proud, but I hope you can see the effort, the commitment, and the love that I put into everything I do, mirroring the example you set.

As I raise my sons, I teach them the lessons you taught me through love, hard work, and integrity. Just as you did for me, I strive to prepare them for the world—to be men of character who are kind, strong, and driven.

Thank you for teaching me the importance of wisdom and vigilance in life—that nothing worthwhile comes without effort.

Thank you, Dad, for every sacrifice, every lesson, and every moment of tough love. It has shaped me more than you know.

Dear brother, you are truly fortunate to have good health, which enables you to live life freely and experience its adventures. You've travelled the world with only a backpack and built a successful health and fitness empire in Limpopo with over a dozen gyms. Your hard work and achievements fill me with immense pride.

Remember our harrowing microlight flight, when the engine failed and you skilfully crash-landed, ensuring our survival? That moment truly exemplifies your ability to take the reins and persevere.

Growing up with two brothers with haemophilia, you often played a supportive role, but you never avoided the responsibilities or hard work of being a healthy sibling. Your strong mindset and leadership abilities stand out, especially during brotherhood lodge meetings, where your ideas and status are highly respected.

Your fearless spirit—whether skydiving or bungee jumping—inspires me deeply. The way you embrace life's hurdles with a no-fear attitude is something I admire and aspire to emulate. You are a testament to living a life of courage and adventure, proving time and again that with a positive outlook, one can overcome even the most daunting obstacles.

Surviving a plane crash with your daughter is a reminder of the second chances life gives us. It's a testament to the enduring spirit of love, forgiveness, and success that defines you.

Thank you for being more than just a brother. I appreciate the life lessons you have taught me about hard work, persistence, and enjoying life. Here's to your continued success and happiness.

May your future be granted even greater achievements and deeper fulfilment. You have shown me that true strength is about facing life head-on, and for that, I am endlessly grateful.

You and I had different experiences growing up. I was influenced by our dad's time in the police force, while you were shaped by our family business. It's incredible to see how much you've achieved, taking over the business and elevating it to new heights. Your knack for negotiation ensures that no one takes advantage of you, qualities that command my respect and admiration.

I am deeply grateful for the honour of officiating your wedding to Solana. It was a truly special moment for me, symbolising not just your union but the strength of our family ties. We spent years not talking due to misunderstandings and envy. I was envious of the close relationship you had with our dad. Those years also brought on a spiritual awakening for me, helping me understand that each of us has our own unique path to follow. I'm thankful that we've been able to forgive each other and are now rebuilding our bond, step by step.

Everyone jokes about how much we look alike—even some ex-girlfriends have noticed! You've grown to resemble Zac Efron while I joke about turning into Bud Spencer. Keep in mind that you possess all the essential qualities for immense success as your business empire grows: a compassionate nature, powerful leadership abilities, and unwavering determination.

You make me proud, and I am honoured to be your brother. Keep reaching for the stars, knowing that your big heart and bold spirit are your greatest assets. Here's to more success, love, and laughter in the years to come.

Dear Tiaan,

To my oldest son, my champ, you have taught me more about life than you could possibly imagine. Your old drawing inspired the hug we shared with the world. It taught us about love and connection, and I hold that memory dear. You possess a gentle and wise spirit that belies your years, qualities that make me immensely proud.

Life has thrown us curveballs, notably when your mom and I divorced. This changed our family dynamic significantly, and I regret that it meant seeing you mostly during the holidays. Despite this, you and your brother remain my greatest motivation, my pride, and my joy. You are the reason I continue to push forward, never giving up on the promise of tomorrow.

I hope that one day you will climb Kilimanjaro and have the same life-changing experience that I had. It is a journey that can help you find and live your true purpose.

Tiaan, never stop pursuing your dreams. Put in the work, continue learning, and never stop improving yourself. You are no longer just my little boy; you are a young gentleman with the strength to face anything life throws your way.

Remember that you are a firewalker—you can overcome any obstacle. Difficult experiences are meant to make you stronger and help you become the powerful person I see in you. Build your legacy, create lasting memories, and always carry the knowledge that you are loved deeply. I believe in you, now and always.

My youngest son, my champion, from the moment you decided to come four weeks early, you showed the world your strong spirit. At just two years old, you fearlessly walked on fire, broke boards, and accomplished remarkable feats. Challenges have never intimidated you. It pains me deeply that I wasn't there during many moments of your young life. You grew up wondering why Mom left and had to get to know me in short spurts, primarily during holidays. For this, my son, I am deeply sorry.

Your resilience and strength will continue to inspire and challenge me every day. You possess a remarkable tenacity that assures me you are destined for great heights. Your struggles will help you become someone who can help others in a meaningful way. Your courage is boundless, and your heart remains tender despite the hardships.

Know that I love you deeply and am immensely proud of you. I encourage you, just as I did your brother, to one day climb Kilimanjaro. It's a journey that transformed me, and one I believe could help you forge your own path and build your legacy. I hope you can find it in your heart to forgive my absences and understand that, despite them, my love for you has never lost its strength.

If you flip to the back of the book, then you've seen the public version of who I am, but that barely scratches the surface. In the rest of this book, you'll meet the real Cobus Visser at his most vulnerable.

I was going to write this book in 2018, after I'd summited Stella Point (5756 m) on Mount Kilimanjaro, Africa's highest mountain (5895 m). It never happened. I kept telling myself I'd write it, and I never did.

To be honest, I felt like a failure for not getting to Uhuru, the highest part of the mountain. Stella Point, Gilman's Point, and Uhuru Peak are three official summit points on Mount Kilimanjaro. The true summit is called Uhuru Peak. Stella Point and Gilman's Point are lower points located along the crater rim. So, I thought, "Who wants to read about someone who didn't reach his goal?" But, as I reflected, I realised that it was still a massive achievement and worth writing about.

But if I'd written it in 2018, however, it would only have been about my Kilimanjaro experience. I've had time to reflect on my life and what came before Kilimanjaro and surely after.

I've had time to reflect on all those people that impacted my life and got me from there to here.

My father, Theunis Visser, asked me why I wanted to write a story about myself when I'm so young (41).

I suppose this question is as good as any place to start. Simply put, I may not be around tomorrow to write my story. One brain bleed could mess up all my plans. I wanted to leave some kind of legacy that my family, friends, and others could learn from. I would have loved to have read my grandfather's story. As the first president of South Africa, he lived a large life. But he didn't leave a story for me to read, which is a pity. I'm leaving my story, and maybe it means something to someone.

I was born with an inherited bleeding disorder called haemophilia. I could bleed out at any time; I don't have any elbows or ankles to speak of, and I'm in constant pain.

This disorder has been damaging, not only to me but also to those who have supported me. There have been times that I wish I could end it all. I'd actually decided to tap out in 2018 on Mount Kilimanjaro. I knew I wasn't coming back. Of course, man plans, and God laughs. He brought me back from the mountain, changed and reborn. He had other plans for me, which I'm still trying to fathom.

I can only believe that by writing this book, I still have a purpose, and I'm not done yet.

It hasn't been easy for me to hang on, and this book has given me a project that could keep me alive for a little longer. I heed the words of pastor Rick Warren: "If you're alive, there's a purpose for your life." I'm starting to believe this to be true.

2023–2024 has not been an easy time for me. Tapping out has again been on my mind. I am writing this book at a period of my life where I have been reflecting on what I've been facing. I've come off a couple of heartbreaking relationships and have lost six people who were close to me in this time. I've also been in a dark place and have been struggling with the black dog of depression.

This book project has given me a new zest for life and given me a reason to live. I didn't give up on Kilimanjaro, and it became my saving grace. This book might just be that for me too.

I don't know how this book will land for you. I'm hoping that it will have some impact because of the things I share with you. Perhaps it will make you cry, and perhaps you'll hate me because my imperfection (of character) has laid waste to some of my relationships.

I'm writing this book to atone for some people I've hurt—my ex-wife, Mar-nelle in particular. I'm hoping that this book leaves some kind of legacy for my sons and their children. It is my hope that they read this book and realise what their dad (and grandfather) went through. It is my fervent hope that this book will inspire them to forge their own path so that they can leave a beautiful legacy behind.

If I had a definitive goal for this book, it would be to inspire you to do whatever it takes to ensure that you are living your purpose and that you are happy, so that you can live without regret.

In my thirties, I was known as the Superman of Africa. I embraced that brand for a decade.

At the beginning of 2022, I facilitated a firewalk for 100 people. It was an exhilarating start to the year, and the event was met with enthusiasm and positive feedback. However, just a week later, I faced an unexpected setback. During a follow-up with the client, I was shocked to learn they were dissatisfied with the event—my first client disappointment in ten years. They expressed that they would not work with me again. This feedback sent me into a spiral of self-doubt.

In response, I decided to take proactive steps to rediscover and reinforce my skills. By February, I had revisited courses that had originally shaped my career, such as Mind Power, Sales Explosion, and UPW Online, as well as an NLP refresher. These courses reminded me of my foundational principles and reignited my passion for what I do. During this period of introspection and learning, I attended a morning workshop with Mike and Landi Jack, where we immediately connected.

When Mike outlined a 12-month coaching journey with a staggering fee of nearly 350k, I was initially taken aback. However, after discussing it with Krupa, my partner from 2018 to 2020, who also believed in the value of this investment, I committed by paying my deposit and arranging monthly payments.

As the coaching progressed, I realised that I had outgrown my 'Superman' brand. The persona no longer fitted me, both literally and metaphorically (I didn't fit into my Superman suit any more), as I now sported a beard and a belly.

More profoundly, I learned that Superman, as a character, was somewhat of a loner and had a significant vulnerability like Kryptonite. This understanding led me to believe it was time for a change—a rebranding to reflect my evolution and the new decade of my life, as I was about to leave my thirties.

This period of transition coincided with my exploration of Viking culture, which deeply resonated with me. After taking a DNA test that showed that I had roots in northern Germany, Denmark, and Norway, I felt even more connected to this heritage. I admired the Vikings for their fearlessness in battle, strong sense of family and community, faith-driven lives, and legacy of exploration and conquest.

Importantly, Viking society regarded women as equals, and this was foundational in shaping modern Europe. Inspired by their virtues and values, I embraced the Viking ethos in my personal and professional life.

This shift proved to be just as transformative for my business. Adopting a Viking-inspired brand not only rejuvenated my outlook but also resonated with my clients. In 2022, my business had its best year ever. It allowed me to fully fund my coaching and opened the door for me to expand globally. The difficulties of the year, while daunting, were pivotal in steering me towards a path of personal growth and professional renewal.

After coming across the Viking culture, I started studying it intently because it resonated so much with my #whateverittakes and #livewithoutregret philosophy.

When I turned 40 on November 2, 2022, I fully embraced the brand and am now known as Cobus 'Viking' Visser.

My foundation, built on the nine values and virtues of the Vikings, embodies a powerful framework for personal and professional development, deeply resonant with my life story and teachings. These values—courage, truth, honour, fidelity, discipline, hospitality, industriousness, self-reliance, and perseverance—work for me; they may just be helpful to you too.

COURAGE

Courage is the ability to confront fear, pain, danger, uncertainty, or intimidation. My journey, especially my ascent of Mount Kilimanjaro despite physical limitations and health challenges, exemplifies unparalleled courage. As you've probably heard before, courage is not the absence of fear but the determination to act in spite of it.

TRUTH

Truth involves living with honesty and integrity, not just in words but in actions. I believe that it is important to be authentic and to be true to ourselves and our values.

HONOUR

Honour is a code of conduct that recognises the dignity of individuals and their actions. I honour every person's potential to overcome adversity by celebrating their achievements and encouraging respect for themselves and others.

Fidelity

Fidelity means loyalty and faithfulness to one's principles, family, friends, and community.

Discipline

Discipline is the commitment to consistency, self-control, and excellence. I strive to be disciplined (I don't always get it right).

Hospitality

Hospitality reflects the generosity and friendliness shown to those around us.

Industriousness

Industriousness is the virtue of hard work and perseverance.

Self-reliance

Self-reliance is the ability to depend on one's own capabilities, judgement, and resources.

Perseverance

Perseverance is the steadfastness of doing something despite difficulty or delay in achieving success. I have tried to embody the spirit of never giving up, no matter the obstacles.

I believe that the Viking values offer a robust framework for overcoming adversity, achieving personal growth, and leading a fulfilling and impactful life.

Below are some more Viking traits that appeal to me.

No Fear

The Vikings' approach to life and battle was characterised by a fearless attitude. I believe that #whateverittakes demonstrates that fearlessness is about confronting fears head-on and pushing through barriers.

Travellers

Vikings were explorers at heart, navigating uncharted territories. Clearly, I was a Viking before I knew it. I've travelled to more than 20 countries at this stage of my journey.

Community-Focused

Community was central to Viking life. I place a high value on community and brotherhood, fostering a backing of networks and emphasising the power of collective effort and unity in achieving goals.

Gender Parity

Vikings respected women's roles in society, recognising their strength and contributions. I champion equality and empowerment for all.

Faith

Faith played a significant role in Viking life, guiding their actions and beliefs. My journey is underpinned by a deep faith in God and in the resilience of the human spirit.

Tenacity and Grit

The Vikings' legendary strength and resilience are qualities that I embody and encourage in others. My life story is a testament to overcoming physical and emotional adversities through inner strength and determination.

Freedom

Freedom was a core Viking value, seen in their adventurous spirit and way of life. I believe that we should live a life of freedom, pursue our passions, live authentically, and make choices that align with their true selves. I left a thriving and safe furniture business to follow my passion.

Embody Whatever It Takes

Vikings did whatever was necessary to thrive and conquer. My philosophy of #whateverittakes reflects this determination, emphasising the importance of commitment, resilience, and taking decisive action to achieve one's goals.

First to Sail the Unknown

Vikings were pioneers, first to navigate uncharted waters. I try to inspire others to embark on their journeys of self-discovery and personal growth, daring to explore new possibilities and redefine their limits.

Conquerors

The Vikings were renowned for their conquering spirit. I've certainly had my fair share of personal contests to conquer and have tried my best to transform adversities into victories.

The indomitable spirit of Vikings, fighting until the end, resonates with my approach to life's battles. I believe that it's important to persevere, be tenacious, and never give up, no matter the odds.

Despite my challenges with haemophilia and depression, I've had some amazing times and adventures that have made me very happy.

I became known as Africa's Superman (I have an affinity for Clark Kent) because my #whateverittakes and #livewithoutregrets philosophy has allowed me to achieve some rather wonderful and remarkable things in my life.

Some of the highlights of my life are the birth of my two sons, helping my dad build his furniture business into one of the biggest independent chains in South Africa, being the only Master Firewalking Instructor in Africa, speaking in front of an audience of 3 500 people, helping hone the mindsets of both the South West Districts Eagles and Southern Kings provincial rugby teams, walking over fire with 6 500 other people on an Anthony Robbins Unleash the Power Within event in Dallas in 2014, and, of course, climbing Mount Kilimanjaro on crutches in 2018.

I can definitively say that my journey as a professional speaker and firewalking facilitator had its genesis on November 19, 2011, when I attended a financial freedom weekend seminar held by Hannes Dreyer.

Hannes facilitated an arrow-breaking activity as part of the exercises. He held an arrow to my throat and told me to push. I thought that it would pierce me and that there was no way I could survive it. The shaft of the arrow snapped, and I came out totally unscathed and completely changed. Breaking this arrow totally changed my life's trajectory. Facing what felt like certain death and then feeling the release afterwards made me feel as though I had dropped all the baggage I carried with me. Just before this retreat, I wanted to kill myself, but breaking this arrow took my fear away and gave me a profound reason to live.

But there was more to come, and this changed my destiny. Hannes lit a massive bonfire for us in the evening. He then told us that we'd be walking over coals that night. I was incredulous and thought, "There's no way I'm doing this." But as Hannes began to explain the principles behind the practice, I couldn't help but feel a growing sense of curiosity and determination. The fire crackled and spat, casting long shadows on the ground, as I listened intently to what he had to say.

When it came to my turn for a brief moment, I wanted to run. This was madness, after all. The coals are around 500–600°C. To give you an idea of how hot that is, aluminium melts at around 250°C and one can get third-degree burns at just 150°C.

I took a deep breath, and the last tremor of fear left my body. A calm descended upon me. I raised my head and directed my eyes to my end goal: reaching my friends Ash Cobus Erasmus, Hannes Dreyer, and his wife. I stepped into the fire.

Ash Cobus Erasmus holds a special place in my heart. I met Ash just as I turned 16, and from that moment on, we became brothers.

As I made my way across the fiery path, each step resonated with the strength of my bond with Ash Cobus Erasmus. My brother in spirit stood at the end, his presence a testament to the years of untiring backing he had given me. His encouragement was crucial back in 2013, when he hosted my first firewalk, standing steadfast beside me as I leaned on him for balance, ensuring I didn't falter. That first journey, with my hands on his shoulders, wasn't just about overcoming fear; it was a shared victory, a moment that solidified our lifelong solidarity and mutual resilience.

One of the most significant memories I have of Ash is the day I had the blessing of baptising him at a waterfall in the mountains. This sacred moment not only strengthened our spiritual connection but also symbolised the deep trust and love we have for each other. Ash has always been there for me, especially during pivotal moments in my life. He was my saving angel when I walked on fire for the first time, providing the encouragement I needed to conquer my fears.

Today, Ash lives in New Zealand, but despite the physical distance, we maintain a deep connection rooted in spirituality and shared experiences. Our conversations often get philosophical, and I am forever grateful and honoured to know him. His belief in me after all these years has been a constant source of strength.

In a lighthearted yet touching promise, Ash once told me that when I become a world leader or the UN president, he would be my personal bodyguard. This playful vow underscores the depth of our bond and the faith we have in each other's potential.

I walked 12 times that night. Neither a burn nor a blister were in sight. I was so excited about the experience that I didn't sleep at all.

It was that night that I decided to become a firewalking instructor so that I could help release the potential in others the way it had opened up in me.

At the seminar, Hannes read a quote by Og Mandino that he said had a major impact on his life. It irrevocably changed my life and is today tattooed on my heart.

"I AM HERE FOR A PURPOSE AND THAT PURPOSE IS TO GROW INTO A MOUNTAIN, NOT TO SHRINK TO A GRAIN OF SAND. HENCEFORTH, WILL I APPLY ALL MY EFFORTS TO BECOME THE HIGHEST MOUNTAIN OF ALL AND I WILL STRAIN MY POTENTIAL UNTIL IT CRIES FOR MERCY."

OG MANDINO

I decided then that I was going to learn as much as I could about mindset and human potential. This led me to attend a Mind Power Seminar by John Kehoe and Robin Banks. Nothing was the same after that seminar.

At that time, Anthony Robbins was running firewalks for thousands of people through his UPW (Unleash the Power Within) events and other interventions. I Googled everything that I could about Anthony Robbins—and about firewalking.

One name kept popping up: Tolly Burkan. They call him the father of firewalking. He created the world's first firewalking course in 1977. He taught these techniques to many celebrities, including Andrew Weil, M.D., Regis Philbin, T. Harv Eker, and Anthony Robbins.

In 2012, I attended Firewalking Instructor Training (FIT) in Dallas, Texas. There were five other delegates from the United States, Mexico, Peru, and Dubai. The training was led by master instructor Charles Horton and his team. I thought I might get to meet Tolly Burkan, who has since retired. But I didn't. I am, of course, forever grateful that he created this amazing process.

On that particular weekend, I bravely conquered the scorching flames not once, not twice, but an astounding 125 times. To graduate, we each had to walk 108 times over a length of 250 metres. I never got burned once. It was brilliant.

We didn't only learn how to firewalk. We learned how to break boards, break bricks, break arrows, walk over glass, bend rebars, and put a needle through our hands.

The instructors said that I could sit out some of the sessions because they were mindful that I am a haemophiliac and that any of these activities could prove dangerous. I, of course, declined and participated in everything. I felt some trepidation about having to break a board. My elbow is, at the very least, challenging. I was terrified that I could disintegrate it and lose its use entirely. I broke the board. It was lifechanging. I thought, "If you can do this, you can do anything."

I walked through broken glass with not so much as a scratch. Yet another resounding triumph. Walking on broken glass was an intimidating and scary experience. Being a heavy guy at 120 kg, hearing the glass crack under my weight heightened my anxiety. The 8-metre path ahead felt like an interminable test. Yet, as I took each step, I not only overcame the physical test but also silenced the little voices of doubt in my head. This experience taught me a powerful lesson about confronting and conquering my fears, transmuting what initially seemed daunting into a profound personal victory.

In another process, we had to stick a needle through our hand without bleeding. Most of the people were a bit squeamish. As a haemophiliac, I have had so many needles stuck into me that this was a breeze. We had to chant, "My body is a river. My body is space." Over and over again. The needle went through, and there was no blood. The power of the mind is amazing.

Weirdly, the biggest quandary for me was the sweat lodge. We all had to get naked to participate. My Christian upbringing made me uncomfortable with it, but I did it in the end, and it was the most freeing experience.

Stripping down proved to be quite challenging. I have always been uncomfortable with my body, feeling particularly vulnerable in such exposed moments. The inability to go to the gym due to my physical limitations often left me feeling inadequate, especially after being trolled on social media for my 'little arms and big belly,' and that I should get into exercising with cruel comments from those unaware of my struggles. They didn't know how much I wished to look like Arnold Schwarzenegger. Yet, here I was, stripping down for a spiritual sweat lodge. It was a meaningful redirection towards me starting to love and accept my body and to let go of the hurt. This act became a gateway to connecting with God, helping me to embrace my vulnerabilities and find peace in my own skin.

The only thing I was unable to do was break a brick. That was going a little too far for me. I couldn't do it. If misery loves company, not even the instructor was able to break the brick. I was so disappointed that I cried. I remember thinking, "You'll break this brick; maybe not today, but you'll break this brick." I wiped away my tears and vowed to continue training until I could break it. No matter how many setbacks I faced, my determination remained unshakeable.

I took the brick back to South Africa with me. The customs officials took me off to one side. Perhaps they thought it was a bomb. They couldn't believe that I was carrying a 10-kg brick with me. I told them the story of my failure and said that I wanted to break it at home.

And I did—not the same brick, but I broke one nonetheless. It was when I went as a support instructor to the Spain Executive FIT (EFIT) programme. Part of becoming a FIT Master Instructor was that we had to assist in six FIT training camps.

I became a Master Firewalking Instructor on November 2, 2014, on my birthday in Dallas, Texas.

In February 2014, while on my second EFIT, on my way to becoming a Master, I went to Hawaii's Big Island, which had an active volcano.

One night, we were instructed to go for a walk on lava. Just the thought of it sent terror spiralling through my body.

We started out at 09h00. It was raining, and we walked through endless mud. It was tough going. Every time you took a step, you'd sink in deep, sometimes right to your hips. So, if you stepped wrong, someone had to help you out. It was physically and mentally exhausting.

It was almost night-time, and I just couldn't go on anymore. The problem was that you couldn't sit down because the gases from the lava would make you sleep. And if you slept, you died. I never did get to experience walking on lava that night, but all my fellow trainers did. The walk back was a nightmare. I think we started out at 22h00 to get back to our base. Everyone passed me. I realised then that when it gets tough and survival is paramount, most people will only think about themselves. As a side note, the place where we camped no longer exists. It was swept away by lava a few years later.

When we got to camp, I couldn't sleep. I was in so much pain. I had to crawl to the shower. I had to crawl outside to clean my only pair of walking shoes. I couldn't walk. I couldn't walk the next day. So much so that I even got a mention in Charles Horton's book, Ignite the Secret (chapter 11):

"It was at this point that I came upon Cobus. He is a haemophiliac. Because of this condition, his wrists and ankles don't work quite right. Yet I had seen him firewalk, walk on broken glass, and break boards and bricks—not once, but seven times each—to become a FI.R.E. Master Instructor—and now he had been walking for ten hours straight, through the rainforest and on a volcano.

Upon reaching Cobus, I went from holding a bitter silence to streaming a constant rush of tears. I'm reasonably healthy, and I had pushed my body far beyond what seemed possible. Imagine what he had been going through! I am so proud of Cobus—a true Superman. He pushed me out of my comfort zone and beyond the point at which I thought I had to give up. He reminded me that I had promised myself never to give up. Somehow, I pushed on.

At 01h00, eleven hours after starting that gruelling walk, I finally got back to the van. I had been crying for an hour or more, and I had no tears left. My body was shaking badly. I was caked in mud from head to toe. I grappled to get my shoes off and discard them on the ground.

Sitting in the van, waiting for others to arrive, I sat in silence amid the buzz of conversation, still not ready to respond to anyone. Finally, irritated by all the noise, I gathered the energy to utter my first words in several hours: "Shut. Up."

After ten minutes of silence, someone started laughing. It became contagious, and soon all of us were laughing. I thought, "Well, what do you know? I haven't given up after all."

The last participant got in the van at 02h00. He was in the same mental and physical condition I had been suffering through an hour earlier. I said, "You may not believe it now, but soon you will laugh about this."

He just glared at me with eyes that could have killed.

Our entire group had pushed our bodies further than we ever thought we could. Why? Because we had to. We literally had to succeed or die. When you make things a 'must' in your life, you will absolutely accomplish them. We all made it, including Cobus. We never gave up, and to this day, I am so proud of this group. We pushed ourselves further than we thought possible, and the strength we gained from the experience is priceless.

Don't allow yourself to give up on your goals and dreams. When you refuse to give up, you can do unimaginable things."

To date, I have trained more than 150 firewalking instructors across the globe in more than 20 countries, including, New Zealand, Thailand, Singapore, USA, Canada, Slovakia, Hungary, Dubai, Uganda, Kenya, Swaziland, Lesotho, Cameroon, and, of course, South Africa. At every training session, I still walk 108 times across 250 metres of fire. I estimate that I've walked over fire more than 2000 times since

2011. More than 13 000 people have walked across one of my fires.

I facilitated an event in Sandton, Johannesburg, where 3 500 people walked over broken glass. I've had in excess of 3 000 people break boards, 1 000 break arrows, and 250 break bricks. It's been a rush, and I've loved every minute of it.

My deepest gratitude goes to Hannes Dreyer, who put me on this path.

There was, however, a downside or an upside, depending on whether you believe that God does everything for your own good.

Becoming a firewalking instructor is a costly exercise. The initial course in 2012 cost $3 500, excluding travel and accommodation costs. I had to understudy and help out at six other training sessions across the world. The travel and accommodation costs were eye-watering. I estimated that from 2012 to 2014, I spent in the region of R650 000 on firewalking.

Including my firewalking, my coaching course, my NLP course, and other seminars, I estimated that I had dropped R950 000 on these endeavours.

I realised that I'd become addicted to learning, and I'd become a seminar junkie.

The salary I got from our family business couldn't sustain the habit. I took out a second bond on our beautiful 5-bedroom house. I had to start selling everything, until finally I had to move my family to my parents' home in Centurion. From king to pauper in two years. With a mountain of debt. What a comedown.

I've no doubt that this was the straw that broke the camel's back for my long-suffering wife, Mar-nelle. She had to contend with the knowledge that I'd had an affair in 2014 (more about that in a later chapter). We got married in 2005, and there was more 'in sickness' than 'in health,' and now I'd lost everything. She left me just before Christmas in 2017. And I can't say I blame her.

#Whateverittakes

At its core, #whateverittakes represents an unwavering commitment to achieving one's goals, surpassing limitations, and realising one's full potential. It signifies a readiness to confront challenges head-on, to navigate the turbulent waters of change, and to emerge victorious against all odds.

Lessons to Embody: #whateverittakes

No Excuses, Only Actions

I believe that when individuals commit to doing their best, there's an implicit allowance for excuses and blame-shifting. However, embracing #whateverittakes eradicates this allowance, compelling individuals to take decisive action and assume full responsibility for their outcomes.

The Power of Commitment

This philosophy teaches the importance of unwavering commitment. It's about pledging to reach one's goals, regardless of the obstacles that may arise. This commitment is the fuel that drives individuals to keep pushing forward, even when the path ahead seems insurmountable.

Transformation Through Adversity

My own journey illustrates that adversity is not a barrier but a catalyst for growth. #whateverittakes is about leveraging challenges as opportunities to evolve, strengthen one's character, and forge a path to success.

Empowerment and Self-Reliance

By living according to #whateverittakes, individuals learn to rely on their inner strength and capabilities. This mindset empowers them to take control of their destiny, to make impactful decisions, and to become architects of their future.

Legacy of Impact

#whateverittakes is about leaving a lasting impact. The true measure of success is not just in achieving one's personal goals but in inspiring others to pursue their dreams with the same fervour and dedication.

For me, #whateverittakes is more than a slogan; it's a reflection of my life's work and my mission to inspire and empower others. It embodies my belief in the potential of every individual to achieve greatness, to overcome any challenge, and to live a life of purpose and meaning. This philosophy is woven into the fabric of my coaching, speaking engagements, and personal endeavours, serving as a beacon of hope and a call to action for those seeking to completely change their lives.

#whateverittakes is a powerful expression of my philosophy and approach to life. It encapsulates lessons of resilience, commitment, and the relentless pursuit of excellence. By embracing this mindset, individuals can unlock their potential, overcome obstacles, and achieve their dreams, embodying the very essence of living a life without limits.

Embracing the philosophy of #whateverittakes fundamentally intertwines with the concept of living by one's values. This philosophy isn't just about determination; it's a testament to how deeply you hold your principles. Be prepared, as the true test of commitment to your values inevitably approaches.

Remember, choose your words carefully—words are powerful, and once spoken, they invite trials that test their sincerity. Throughout my journey, I've faced numerous tests: some I failed, providing valuable lessons, and others I conquered, reinforcing my resolve. Each challenge, each test, is an opportunity to reaffirm what truly matters to me. As I continue on this path, I realise the importance of resilience and adaptability, ensuring that my actions always align with my deepest convictions, no matter the obstacles I encounter.

#livewithoutregret is not just a phrase for me; it's an insight gleaned from a life-altering experience. This philosophy became especially significant after my journey to Mount Kilimanjaro, an adventure that tested my limits and brought me face-to-face with the fragility of life. On my descent from the summit, I encountered a situation that nearly cost me my life—a moment that crystallised the importance of living fully and without regret.

The Essence of #livewithoutregret

Living without regret means embracing every moment, making choices that align with one's deepest values and desires, and taking action despite fear or uncertainty. It's about recognising that life is a precious, fleeting gift and that every day offers opportunities for growth, joy, and fulfilment.

Here are some key lessons that you may incorporate to #livewithoutregret

Embracing the Present

I believe that we should fully engage with the present, to cherish our experiences, and to appreciate the people in our lives. It's a reminder that the past cannot be changed and the future is not guaranteed, making the present all the more precious.

Bold Decision-Making

Living without regret involves making bold decisions, stepping out of one's comfort zone, and taking risks. It's about pursuing dreams with courage and conviction, knowing that it's better to have tried and failed than never to have tried at all.

Self-Acceptance and Forgiveness

My journey underscores the importance of self-acceptance and forgiveness. Acknowledging that we are enough, forgiving ourselves for our mistakes, and learning from them are crucial steps in living a life without regret.

Pursuing Passion and Purpose

This mindset encourages individuals to discover their passions and to align their actions with their purpose. It's about making meaningful contributions, pursuing activities that bring joy, and living in a way that feels authentic and fulfilling.

Leaving a Legacy

#livewithoutregret is about the legacy we leave behind. I advocate for living in such a way that our actions inspire others, contribute to the betterment of the world, and ensure that our impact is positive and lasting.

#livewithoutregret is a personal mantra, a guiding principle that emerged from a number of near-death experiences and has since informed every aspect of my life. To be honest, there are days when it's challenging to live up to this ideal; it serves as a constant reminder of his commitment to live fully, to embrace my worth, and to make every moment count.

#livewithoutregret is a call to live intentionally, to embrace life's impermanence, and to act in ways that honour our deepest truths. I hope that my life and teachings exemplify this philosophy, inspiring others to live boldly, love deeply, and leave a legacy of positive impact.

My Grandmother and Great-Grandfather

I was in two minds of whether I should put this chapter in. I loved my grandmother dearly, and she influenced me in so many ways. Her stories ignited my love for geography and for the love of travel. Her name was Magdalena Visser, the daughter of CR Swart, South Africa's first president.

He had an indomitable spirit. I think that I got a bit of that. If I look at my father and two siblings, they are all successful in their own right. CR Swart's blood runs deep in all of us.

In 1919, CR Swart sent my grandmother on a journey overseas to Europe, right after the end of the Great War. She embarked on an awe-inspiring adventure that allowed her to immerse herself in the wonders of a whole new world. It took her three months to reach Europe by ship. It was then that she fell in love with travel.

I spent many hours letting her regale me with her amazing travel tales. She travelled to Israel 17 times and to most countries across the globe. This inspired me to travel to Israel in 2006, and I fell in love with Jerusalem. We used to spend endless hours poring over her travel albums.

My grandmother always teased me and said that I'd grow up to be like my grandfather, Charles Robert Swart, who was also known as Oom (uncle) Blackie. "You're as smart as he is. And you're going to be as tall as him," she used to say. He was 2.06 metres tall.

He was smart; there's no doubt about that. He matriculated at 13 and was a qualified lawyer at 17. He later became an advocate.

He was a journalist and a prolific writer. He wrote books, poems, and even songs for the famous Drakensberg Boys Choir. And he even played in a silent movie in Hollywood.

He also fought in the Second Anglo-Boer War, October 11, 1899–May 31, 1902. He was captured and incarcerated in one of the notorious British concentration camps. He was put in front of a firing squad. Luckily for him and us, I suppose, it was a scare tactic, and they released him.

He was the last governor general of South Africa for the British Empire in 1961. When South Africa became a republic in 1961, he became its first president (1961–1969).

Growing up, I always wanted to be like my great-grandfather. At more than two metres tall, he was imposing and charismatic.

My great-grandfather died on July 16, 1982. I hope to one day live up to his legacy.

My Childhood

Theunis Visser: My beautiful baby boy, Cobus, was born on November 2, 1982, in Vereeniging. I was such a proud father. My heart swelled with love as I held him. He was perfect. Until he wasn't.

Three months after his birth, we noticed blue bruises on his body. It was confirmed that he never escaped my wife Ansie's hereditary disease, haemophilia, which can be passed on to sons. He had a 50% chance of getting the disease from his mother, and he never beat the odds. He was a bleeder, and this changed all of our lives irrevocably. We had to make everything safe for him; his knees and arms were covered with sponges, and we handled him gently. We basically wrapped him in cotton wool.

I was a policeman, and Ansie was a housewife in Villiers when he was born.

Cobus was a lovely and loving child, and he captured everyone's heart, from family members to my colleagues at the police station. Everyone was fond of Cobus. He was a very sweet and friendly child. He particularly enjoyed standing on the front or back seat when we drove through town, greeting every person on the street with a wave.

In Reitz, he started his preschool, where he would always make friends with older boys, never with those his own age.

We regularly had to go to the Johannesburg General Hospital's haemophilia clinic for examinations. It was a whole day's affair every month, and Cobus was always calm and composed. One time that must have had a terrible impact on him was when he urgently needed plasma. No vein could be found, and the last resort was to let his head hang off the bed, causing the jugular vein to swell. While in a state of fright, the needle had to be inserted, which was very risky and painful. I can't imagine the fear and pain he must have gone through during that experience. Even then, he was incredibly brave.

Cobus was always a caring child; he just wanted to be friends and never complained if others were mean to him. Cobus loved cricket and rugby and had a broad knowledge of them both.

Cobus Visser: My dad was a police officer (a commander), and he started his career in Villiers. I remember growing up as a young, small child and then moving to Reitz. I grew up in a police environment.

I think it was tough for my father to have a haemophiliac as a son. What must it have been like for him not to be able to really hold me and love me? Every touch could lead to a bruise, or worse, a bleed. At one stage, the teachers at my school thought that I was being abused. He was under a lot of pressure to take care of me because I am a haemophiliac and have a high likelihood of becoming disabled.

I think that created a disconnect between me and my father. He used to play rugby, cricket, and run. He was also the head boy in matric, but he'd never be able to do anything active with me for fear of hurting me.

Both my mom and dad had to sacrifice so much to make sure that I could live the most normal life under the circumstances. I can never repay that debt.

I loved sports but could never partake. I always felt that I let my father down because we couldn't do things together. I felt that he didn't want me. Of course, now I know that he loved me but was afraid to hurt me. It took him 40 years to say the words, "I love you, and I'm proud of you, my son."

In school, I was the quiet one. I often went to school with crutches. It was difficult to explain to people what was wrong with me. Why I bled so easily, why I was often in the hospital, and why I couldn't play sports.

There were some cruel kids who teased me about my affliction. But, on the whole, most of them were kind. School is a rough, rowdy, and physical environment in which I couldn't really partake. But they didn't really know what to do with me or how to handle me. Making it harder to make friends.

However, it turned out that I was actually good at making friends as a child. Even now, I'm good at it. I'm gregarious and empathetic, which generally attracts people to me.

If I remember correctly, most of my friends were older than me. Perhaps they had a level of maturity where they had a sense of what it must have been like to be me. They treated me gently, empathetically, and respectfully.

When I was 14, I remember dating a girl in Grade 12 who was 18. My first girlfriend and first kiss. I remember that she had to make the first move.

As a teenager, I fell in love with movies. I often had to stay at home when I had bleeds in my ankles, knees, or elbows. The movies gave me an escape from the prison that was my body. I loved action movies. This is how I came across Superman, and this character resonated with me to such a point that later, in my business life, I created the Superman persona as a part of my brand.

I identified so much with Clark Kent: meek, awkward, and a bit of a klutz. Even the girl of his dreams, Lois Lane, didn't notice him. He was in stark contrast to the confident and heroic Superman. I dreamt of becoming that hero, having superpowers, and saving people. Weirdly, life imitates art. I have the superpower of walking on hot coals and helping people transform their lives, and I'm a bit of a rescuer; I know it.

Going to church was an important part of my youth. I loved the sense of community and the peaceful atmosphere inside the church. It was a place where I could reflect and find solace in times of uncertainty.

However, I battled when we had services where people prayed for others to be healed. Healing was taking place left, right, and centre, but not for me. I just wanted God to heal me, and He wouldn't. Like with my father, I felt that I wasn't good enough.

In 1996, while on the last day or so of our school holiday, I hit my head on someone else while I was in a swimming pool. When I was at school, I had a severe headache that stretched to a migraine.

I stayed at home the next day. When my mom got home, I got up to greet her and passed out. Every time I got up to move somewhere, I would lose consciousness, only to wake up much later. And, before we knew it, I went into a coma. I had a life-threatening brain bleed. This is the closest I have come to death in my 40 years on this planet.

The next thing I remember is waking up in an ICU. My head was heavily bandaged. I had an operation to stop my brain from swelling more.

I couldn't deal with the pain and frustration of how this unfolded, and I begged and begged with tears streaming down my face for God to take me. I didn't want to live. Of course, He had other ideas.

I was let out of the hospital. The doctor who operated on me didn't close the wound properly, and I started bleeding again. I ended up in the Johannesburg General Hospital, as it was known then (now, it's the Charlotte Maxeke Johannesburg Academic Hospital), where I had to undergo two operations before we got the bleeding under control. As a consequence of these operations, I have damaged brain cells on the right side of my brain.

This became apparent when, in 2017, I passed out while driving my car and collided with another vehicle. I had suffered an epileptic attack. I've been on epilepsy medicine ever since.

It took me three months to recover before I could go back to school. Getting back made it a formidable space to be in, especially after missing nearly half a year. I had a significant amount of catching up to do to stay on track with my classmates in Standard 6 (Grade 8).

The process was exhausting, and I frequently wrestled with a foggy head, making concentration difficult. Although it was hard, I was able to overcome the obstacles and successfully finish the school year thanks to my determination and constant effort.

I've subsequently had two more brain bleeds, one in 2008 and the other in 2015. Fortunately, these were cured with one visit to the hospital for five days and one with just Factor VIII plasma injections.

There was one more incident where I nearly never made it. I call it my night of horror in a hospital.

Around 2003, I was using medication called Vioxx that stopped the pain I was going through. This medication was a miracle because I lived 24/7 in pain, and it took me an hour to get out of bed every day. Vioxx saved my life.

I consulted a physiotherapist, who assisted me in strengthening my elbows. This was necessary because I had received a treatment called radioactive utrum for my joints. This treatment eliminates the tissues around the joints. The combination of radioactive utrum, Vioxx, and creatine that I used to build strength, along with treatment by the physiotherapist, was too much for me.

I started bleeding internally one night, and blood came out everywhere. I went to Charlotte Maxeke Johannesburg Academic Hospital because I couldn't afford a private hospital without medical insurance, and I had just cancelled mine. In the emergency ward, I remember waiting for the nurses to bring blood to me. During the night, drug addicts would come in and rob people.

Some of the beds were full of blood because the sheets weren't changed. I had a friend bring me a big duvet and pillows. I would place my suitcase on the bed and keep my feet over it. Then, I would cover myself and hold onto everything tightly to avoid getting robbed.

It took the nurses a long time and a lot of pleading from me to bring my blood. The thing with a blood transfusion is that it takes time, and you have to do it slowly. But whenever the nurses left, I would open the drip so that it could flow much faster because I couldn't imagine staying another night at the hospital. I remember calling my dad at 21h00 to collect me. Having medical insurance is crucial in South Africa since you definitely want to avoid the unpredictable nature of public hospitals.

In 1989, when I was seven years old (Grade 4), I discovered that I had an aptitude for chess. My dad taught me to play chess. I took to chess like a duck to water. My teacher put me against two kids on the chess team, one middle-ranked and one top-ranked. I beat them both. This was surprising, since I'd only learned how to play chess a month before that.

I was immediately put on the school chess team as number two.

Years later, in 1995, I qualified for the Northwest team to go to the South Africa championship in Durban. Wow, I was excited! I was proud that there was something I excelled at. A snag was that I'd always been near a doctor where I could get my plasma injections. I need to take plasma injections whenever I get a bleed. My parents were trained to give me my injections at home.

If I were at school and I got a bleed, I'd tell my teachers about it, and they would either get me to a doctor or take me home, where my mom could take care of the injection. I was in my room when, at around 23h00, I had an elbow bleed. I knew that I needed to leave that space to find a teacher who could take me to a hospital to be injected.

My elbow was swollen; I couldn't move it, and I was crying from the pain. I didn't want to wake the teachers so late because it would put pressure on them. I had my plasma kit with me.

Luckily, I had seen how my parents mixed the plasma and injected me. I thought I'd give it a go.

I'd never done this before. I was really scared to put the needle in my arm. I was in incredible pain, and it took me 30 minutes to finally inject myself. I had nothing to lose. As providence would have it, I got my vein the first time I tried, and sighed with relief as the plasma coursed through my body and relieved me of the agonising pain. I was on such a high!

I was so excited and so proud that I couldn't sleep. I'd done something I'd never done before. That moment changed everything for me. I had another skill. I could inject myself and take one more step towards becoming independent.

I am grateful for chess. It kept me focused. In 1996 and 1997, I made it to the Limpopo chess team and played in the South African championship.

I never cracked the nod to get into the South African team. But being on a provincial team was good enough for me. It gave me the experience of being good at something, and that did my self-esteem a world of good.

I did well academically, with my grades ranging from 70-90%. My love for geography and history enriched my academic journey. Geography fascinated me as it allowed me to explore the world through maps and atlases, fuelling my imagination about different cultures and landscapes. It was more than a subject; it was a gateway to discovering our planet from the closeness of my classroom.

History was a passion that went beyond interest, consistently earning me a grade of 100%. I was deeply captivated by the stories of the past, the rise and fall of civilisations, and the lessons we could learn from them. The tales of ancient empires and pivotal events resonated deeply with me.

This passion continues to shape my life. Whenever I travel, I dive into the history of each place I visit, exploring museums and historical sites and engaging with locals to understand their heritage. This approach enriches my travel experiences and connects me deeply with the places I visit.

This journey of chess, academics, and health barriers has instilled in me a burning desire to make a difference. I want to empower and inspire others to believe that the impossible is possible. Through my own life and experiences, I aim to show that with determination, faith, and resilience, one can overcome any obstacle and achieve greatness.

By inspiring people to adopt a #whateverittakes mindset, is to live a life rich with fulfilment and devoid of regret. Through my story, I hope to show others that they too can achieve their dreams, no matter how distant they may seem.

As a coach, speaker, and author, I strive to provide tools, strategies, and encouragement to help individuals unlock their potential. By touching one life at a time, I believe we can create a world where more people are living their truth, achieving the extraordinary, and contributing positively to society.

My goal is to be a catalyst for change, helping people break free from their limitations and step into their greatness. By promoting the belief that the impossible is possible, the hope is that my legacy leaves a lasting impact and inspires others to do the same.

Firewalking Takes Me To Rugby

Dreams can come true, though perhaps not always in the ways we initially envision. I've always loved rugby. And I've always dreamed of playing the game. It's essential to maintain faith and continue to pursue your dreams with determination, even if the odds are stacked against you. My dream of playing rugby didn't go quite like I planned, but it came to life in a way that perhaps set me up to fulfil a higher purpose.

However, as a haemophiliac with shot elbows and ankles, the door that opens to other young, healthy South Africans was shut to me. Either way, God works in miraculous ways, and when the path changes, we can still achieve great results. Later in life, I got to spend time on a rugby field with both the South Western Districts Eagles in 2015 and the Southern Kings in 2017–2018.

I will always treasure the following letter from the current assistant coach to the Springboks, Deon Davids.

Our paths have crossed twice in the rugby world. Both times were exceptional experiences with revealing outcomes.

In 2015, I first heard about you by chance from a friend (Dudley Janeke) at a barbeque in the scenic fishing village of Arniston, and I contacted you the following week. The reason was to help the SWD team, as I had just been appointed Director of Coaching, with the preseason programme. I felt that the group of players was blessed with exceptional talent, but the culture needed to change with the main goal of establishing trust in each other.

We crammed a week's worth of ideas into two days. The interactive activities pushed everyone out of their comfort zones, which was necessary, and set us all on a journey that resulted in a wonderful season filled with success.

In 2017, in my second year as Super Rugby Coach for the Kings and my first opportunity to have a preseason programme with them, I did not hesitate to involve you again. Although not everyone was convinced it was necessary, knowing you and what you could do, I had no doubts about my decision. The rest is history. The testimony lies in the experience of the players, the management, and the coaches and the impact it had on the success of the season, as well as the careers of the players.

Today, Lindsay Weyer (a technical analyst), Konrad von Hagen, and I are World Cup champions. Makazole Mapimpi is a double World Cup winner. Players like Louis Schreuder became a Springbok after his career started at the Kings, and players like Andisa Ntsila, Chris Cloete, and Lionel Cronjé played for the SA A team. Many others, like Irné Herbst, Wilhelm van der Sluys, Wandile Mjekevu, Mike Willemse, Tyler Paul, Ross Geldenhuys, and Malcolm Jaer, have successfully continued their careers overseas and at other local unions.

Even coaches like Dave Williams and Barend Pieterse have been successfully employed at overseas and local unions and national teams.

Thank you for your exceptional contribution to this success. Even more importantly, thank you for the exceptional person you are. You are an example of someone who not only 'talks the talk' but also 'walks the walk.'

Whatever it takes, brother!!

COACH DD (DEON DAVIDS)

SPRINGBOK ASSISTANT COACH AND HEAD COACH OF THE SOUTHERN KINGS

The South West District Eagles played in the Second Division Curry Cup. I facilitated a two-day event for them, stayed with them for the season, and did one-off sessions before some of their games.

I put them through the wringer and got them to participate in a number of processes, including firewalking, walking over broken glass, drumming, board breaking, and rebar bending.

After that, they went from a six-game losing streak to a six-game winning streak to get into the 2015 Curry Cup first division finals in Potchefstroom, only to lose by 44 to 20 to a rampant Leopards team.

In 2017, the Southern Kings were the weakest team in the Super Rugby Championships. They'd only won three games in 2013 and two games in 2016 when Deon invited me to help them out. I played a small part in the journey that unfolded for them. The time we spent at our training camp at the beginning of 2017 in Port Alfred laid the foundation for an amazing season.

They beat South Africa's top two teams that year: the Blue Bulls at Loftus in Pretoria, and then the Sharks, who were at full strength with all their Springboks in front of a crowd of 45 000 people.

They beat the New South Wales Waratahs, and they were the only South African team to beat the Jaguars in Argentina. They lost two games by only one point. If they'd won those games, they would have been in the quarterfinals, and who knows where that would have taken them.

Like with the South West District Eagles, I got them to participate in various team-building activities.

However, for them, it was neither the firewalking nor the arrow exercise that was the most difficult. It was participating in a heart-to-heart hug. After all the players hugged each other, we faced an exercise that felt deeply personal for many of us—imagine giving 45 heart-to-heart hugs in a setting where such displays of affection are not the norm. This isn't a space often looked at for its vulnerability.

But something happened to every person present. It was particularly striking when our eighth man stood to share his experience. His usual reserve was evident when he admitted, "I don't even let my mom get this close to me." Something had shifted for him. "However, boys, today my heart is pumping chocolates for all of you." We all instantly felt better. A deep change took place in our relationships, proving that some awkward moments can surely bring us closer together.

I was exposed to a book by Sara Childre called The Hidden Power of the Heart. Through that, I started looking at the work of the HeartMath Institute. I was fascinated by what I learned. The heart has an innate intelligence and is emotionally aware.

One of the team building exercises I developed in my career was the heart-hug. Hugging and other forms of touch can have many positive effects on our health. Research has shown that hugs can lower heart rate and blood pressure, reduce depression and anxiety, boost the immune system, and even alleviate pain.

Hugging, cuddling, and even handholding can release endorphins and hormones such as serotonin and oxytocin, which are associated with feelings of happiness and bonding. It's incredible how something as simple as a hug can have such profound effects on our overall well-being.

The heart-hug is one of the most powerful exercises in my facilitation arsenal. I've done it with hundreds of people of different cultures from around the world.

I frequently discuss the power of hugs, emphasising the concept of the 'Intentional Hug.' This type of hug isn't just a routine embrace; it's a deliberate act of connection that carries deeper significance. The main idea of intentional hugging is to focus on understanding and meeting the needs of the person you are hugging, rather than focusing on yourself. You never know who might need it the most. Heart-to-heart, leaning to the right, and really holding space for the person you are hugging ignites a transformation that you cannot go back from. Here, the gap between two people is truly bridged.

The practice of the intentional hug should ideally start with family, making it a regular part of life at home. This helps create a culture of affection and understanding in close relationships, which can then extend to others.

When introducing this concept to others, I like to ask, "Can I teach you the Fire Intentional Hug?" This invitation not only piques interest but also opens the door for a meaningful exchange. Here are the steps to effectively give an intentional hug:

Always start by asking if the other person is comfortable receiving a hug. This respects their personal space and sets the tone for a consensual and safe interaction.

Eyes are often described as the windows to the soul, making eye contact a vital part of this profound connection. When I look into your eyes, I truly see you, much like the Na'vi greeting in the movie Avatar. This moment of recognition and acknowledgment is also beautifully captured in the isiZulu word 'Sawubona,' which translates to 'I see you.'

Hugging heart-to-heart also symbolises love and life. I get people to hug so that the left side of each person's heart is touching.

Then, while you hug, you breathe in and out together three times. The brain releases serotonin after just two seconds.

As you gently pull away, maintain eye contact, and express gratitude upon release. This could be a simple 'thank you' or a more personalised acknowledgement of the moment shared.

This closure reinforces the intention behind the hug and leaves both parties feeling valued and respected.

By incorporating these steps into your daily interactions, intentional hugs become a powerful tool for creating deeper connections and spreading positivity.

Selling heart-hugging to a team of rugged men was quite the test. But, being good sports, they went along with it. I believe that this exercise helped them build deeper connections with each other. I believe that this helped them cement their relationships as a band of brothers.

I come with a warning. If you ever meet me, you're probably going to get a heart hug.

Hugging revolutionised my relationship with my son, Tiaan.

When Tiaan was born, the wave of emotion that hit me as I entered the hospital was overwhelming. Due to my physical limitations, I couldn't pick Tiaan up, let alone hold him. This was very hard for me.

As he got older, I couldn't play with him, do rough activities, or teach him how to ride a bike. The barrier affected our relationship and made the early years feel incomplete and disconnected. The things most fathers take for granted became my greatest challenges and deepest regret.

I realised how not being able to interact with me like a son should affected him.

Tiaan, who was four at the time, was drawing a picture that depicted two babies, a girl and a boy. As I watched him draw, he drew a cross over the girl. I asked him why he crossed out the girl baby. He said that he wanted a brother who could play with him because I couldn't. He then showed me another part of his artwork where I was crossed out. Beside it, the words, "Dad, you are dead to me."

That moment changed my life, giving me a painful realisation of how my health impacted my relationship with my son.

What transformed our relationship, however, was something as simple yet as powerful as a hug. It helped heal past hurts and brought us closer emotionally. While I could do very little with Tiaan physically, I could hug him.

I remember the first time I shared this story publicly. Tiaan, who was in the audience, came up to me and hugged me. He asked for my forgiveness, admitting he was young and didn't realise how his words would impact me. I assured him that his honesty catalysed my drive to make a difference in others' lives. Without that moment, I may not have realised my mission to teach the power of connection through small acts such as hugging. That embrace became 'our hug,' cherished and continued even as he navigated his teenage years.

On this journey, Tiaan once asked me if he should follow in my footsteps when he grew up. I was touched by his consideration, but his next words were even more poignant: "Dad, if it's okay with you, may I follow my heart and dreams instead?"

The question emphasised the main thing I had learned and wanted to share: the significance of pursuing one's own path. I encouraged him, filled with pride, to pursue his own passions, just as I had learned to follow mine.

This exchange strengthened our bond and reaffirmed the values of understanding that I deeply cherish as a father. I'm learning and growing alongside my sons, supporting their unique paths with love and openness.

Every time I meet my sons, the first thing they do is ask me to look into their eyes—they're eager for their hug. This ritual has become a cherished part of our reunions, symbolising the reconnection and the healing of past wounds.

I am eternally grateful for these moments. The ability to hug them and hold them close means everything to me. It's a physical manifestation of our love and the progress we've made in rebuilding our relationship. These hugs show that I am there for my children as their father, no matter what happens.

Tiaan, when he was six years old, showed me a drawing that represented the deep impact of our healing and connection. When he was four years old, his artwork symbolically showed me as 'dead', representing the emotional distance between us at that time. This time, however, his drawing told a different story. With a bright smile, he handed me the picture and said, "Dad, I just want to say: you are alive."

Our special connection ritual played a pivotal role in this transformation. Each hug slowly repaired the cracks in our relationship, bringing back his trust in me as both his father and someone who actively loves and takes part in his life. A simple hug can bring life back to distant and strained relationships by showing affection and understanding, even in times of pain.

Journey To Mount Kilimanjaro

In November 2014, I left my family's furniture business, Furn4u/Modern Living, to pursue a career as a firewalking instructor and professional speaker. At that time, I had no plans to climb Mount Kilimanjaro.

Making it to Mount Kilimanjaro in 2018 was a miracle in itself. From 2014 to 2018, my life was fraught with opposition.

My elbows and ankles constantly hurt, keeping me in a wheelchair or on crutches most of the time.

When I left the furniture business, my father was furious because he felt that I'd let the family down. My then wife, Marnelle, and I had helped my dad grow the business from six stores to 27. Currently, it is one of South Africa's largest independent furniture stores, with 37 stores and over 300 employees.

Leaving the family business was a decision laden with emotional weight, especially for my dad. His primary motivation for building the business was to provide a secure future for me and my brother Riaan, both of us being haemophiliacs. In South Africa, my father saw the business as a safeguard for us, protecting us from the difficulties of job hunting with our condition.

This was more than a business strategy; it was my dad's purpose, his 'why', that drove every business decision he made. He openly told us and others that he wanted the business to be our legacy, a place where we could succeed without having to do physical work.

I know that my leaving cut him to the bone.

He was heartbroken that I left my younger brother, Riaan, to cope with the business. There was a massive rift between my father and me, and we didn't speak to each other for almost three years. We've both mellowed and grown since then, and the rift has almost healed completely.

In hindsight, it was the best thing for Riaan and the business. Riaan is now the managing director of Furn4u and Modern Living and has made a massive success out of it. That is his destiny, not mine.

The furniture business wasn't my dream. Initially, I was drawn to the potential of it, envisioning a future where we might build an empire akin to the likes of the Ruperts and Oppenheimers. However, as time passed, it became evident that my father and I did not share the same vision. This misalignment was compounded by the challenging dynamics within our family. No matter how innovative or strategic my ideas were, they never seemed quite right in my father's eyes.

Worse still, when my brother Riaan would suggest the same ideas, they would suddenly be embraced as excellent. This repeated pattern left me feeling undervalued and misunderstood.

Despite being frustrating, these experiences pushed me towards a new path where I could follow my own dream. I discovered a new path in firewalking that allowed me to inspire and uplift others, giving them hope and spreading love. I didn't just change careers; it was a significant gear-shift towards pursuing a personal calling that reflected my values and aspirations. By embracing firewalking, I found a powerful way to help others conquer their fears and obstacles, just like I did. This marked the start of a journey where I could make a real impact, combining my career with my true passions.

Mar-nelle and I moved to a huge mansion in Pretoria with our two sons, Tiaan and Wihan. The house had five bedrooms and three bathrooms. However, in December of 2014, our family faced a significant life change. We left behind our dream house to settle into a modest one-bedroom space in our Visser family house in Pretoria.

We all had to make a big change. Our sons, Tiaan and Wihan, had to get used to sleeping on the ground. All of us were crowded into one room. Adapting to our new environment was a test for our family, requiring a lot of adaptions.

I remember waking up one morning, and I couldn't walk. My ankles were in such pain. As a haemophiliac, I have to take Factor VIII plasma (haemosolvate) to help clot the blood. After getting an injection, it usually takes a day or two for me to be able to use my elbow and ankle joints, and walk normally again.

At first, a short period of feeling unwell turned into weeks, then months, and eventually a year had gone by. My condition deteriorated to the point where I was bedridden, struggling with even the simplest tasks. Mobility became a dream as I crawled to move around our home. Getting to the toilet or into the bath turned into a daily battle. Most nights were spent either in pain, crying myself to sleep, or both. My family put a bed in front of the TV to cheer me up and to make things feel more normal.

The future seemed increasingly bleak when the doctors delivered their prognosis after examining my X-rays. They recommended fusing both of my ankles—a procedure made necessary by my weight and youth, which ruled out replacements. Additionally, both my elbows needed to be replaced. This was the beginning of a daunting two-year journey filled with surgeries and recovery. In October 2016, the date was set for my first operation, which, to this day, never took place.

My mobility was restricted to a wheelchair or crutches. I felt like I had fallen from a king to a pauper. I couldn't walk or work, and I was lost in uncertainty and physical pain.

At the time, firewalking was not popular in South Africa, so it was difficult to find work. And it was even more difficult to run firewalking events in a wheelchair.

The idea faced off with a country that is very religious, and many people saw it as a risky stunt instead of understanding its symbolic importance for personal empowerment.

To make ends meet, I had to work tirelessly. I had to work hard to convince companies to try firewalking. I also had to take on other work, like coaching and training, to make money. It was a relentless hustle, but one driven by a deeper conviction.

During this time, one particular piece of scripture became my anchor and source of strength: Isaiah 43:2 says, "When you walk through the fire, you will not be burned; the flames will not set you ablaze."

This verse is often cited for its assurance of God's presence and protection in times of trouble. No matter how difficult our circumstances are, whether they are as overwhelming as a flood or as painful as a fire, God promises to guide and protect us. We are never alone, even in the darkest of times.

This verse reminded me that my journey was not just about business success but about fulfilling a spiritual calling. I felt relieved knowing that, even with everything going on, I was on the right track. God had a plan for me and was guiding and protecting me.

My faith was alive, and it burned as fiercely as the coals I walked on. My career has always mirrored my firewalking experiences, demonstrating my unwavering faith and strength of conviction. I believed in this prophecy, and it gave me the determination to share the life-changing experience of firewalking when and how I could. I was confident that I would walk through fire without getting burned because I was not alone. God had my back.

Before we knew it, the money ran out, and we were in trouble. Mar-nelle had to find a job to take care of us because my firewalking business was not succeeding. This strained our relationship significantly.

Thanks to my mom, we ended up moving into my parents' house in Centurion in 2015, where we stayed for a year. In 2017, my heart broke as Mar-nelle left me, taking our children to Jefferies Bay. I moved back with my parents in 2018. I still reside there today.

In 2015, two remarkable individuals, Malcolm Moodley and Romy Chanee, became a part of my journey. They arrived at a pivotal moment, like angels sent with a purpose. Both Malcolm and Romy quickly became enamoured with the concept of firewalking and saw the potential impact it could have. They came to me with a proposal. They would handle all the logistics and make sure the fire was safe at every event. This would allow me to focus on what I do best: speaking and inspiring others.

Our collaboration was nothing short of metamorphic. As a team, Malcolm and Romy helped me reach and change many lives without getting stuck in the operational aspects of our workshops. They helped me focus on connecting with people on a deep level and guiding them through the reformative experience of firewalking.

Though our partnership only lasted until 2018, the seasons we shared were filled with growth and mutual learning. We ended our professional relationship with the understanding that sometimes paths diverge, even after greatly contributing to each other's lives.

Malcolm and Romy were instrumental during a crucial phase of my journey, and their legacy within my career cannot be replicated. They were more than just partners; they were integral in helping me navigate a period of significant expansion and impact. I look back on our time together with immense gratitude for their dedication and the deep connection we shared. Their presence showed that people enter your life for a reason and can leave a lasting impact.

This is probably as good a time as any to speak about Mar-nelle and me.

Mar-nelle and I were married on May 14, 2005. I was 22, and she was 23. Our first son, Tiaan, was born on November 11, 2009, and our second son, Wihan, was born on March 28, 2014.

Mar-nelle was my rock and suffered through everything I did. When I was ill, as I often was, she had to take up the reins and make sure that we got through things. She was fiercely determined, loyal, and amazing. Mar-nelle was more than just a partner; she was the cornerstone of my life. She was always there for us, offering unquestionable guidance during the hardest times. Her determination and loyalty kept our family strong and united, helping us overcome every crisis we faced. Her strength was the scaffold of our lives, holding everything together when I could not.

Despite her pivotal role, I admit that I often took her presence for granted. Sometimes, I wish she had challenged my impulsive, emotionally driven decisions that bore significant consequences for our family. She always believed in me without questioning my choices, showing unwavering faith in me.

In the beginning, her steadfastness was the glue that held us together through thick and thin. But as time went on, despite— or perhaps because of—her steadfast nature, we found ourselves drifting apart. This slow separation is just how relationships change, but it is of even greater importance to recognise that a level of mutual understanding is always necessary, not just during hard times but throughout life.

She's seen me through my worst. My haemophilia, and all the drama that goes with that, Hepatitis C in 2012, and when I was diagnosed with depression and epilepsy in 2016. Ultimately, she's seen me through everything. She's seen my pain.

Hepatitis C is a form of viral hepatitis transmitted through infected blood, causing chronic liver disease. Seriously, one of my blood transfusions was infected. How much more do you want to load on me, God? My doctor tells me that I either need a liver transplant or I'll need to go on chronic treatment forever.

After researching the condition, I found this information. It's pretty grim, and it feels like a Sword of Damocles hanging over my head. And that's besides the potential for brain bleeds.

The doctor said it was active and that I needed treatment, or I would have to get a liver transplant, which would change my life forever.

LIVER SCARRING (FIBROSIS). Chronic hepatitis C infection often causes liver fibrosis. This effect may last a long time after treatment. Even if you have little apparent fibrosis, drinking alcohol may worsen the scarring, just as alcohol causes liver damage in people without chronic hepatitis C.

INFECTION RELAPSE. It's possible, but rare, for a hepatitis C infection to reappear after an apparently successful treatment. Relapses usually occur in the first few months after blood testing to confirm that the virus is no longer detectable. Sometimes, however, a relapse becomes evident much later. Although the exact cause of relapse is unknown, the remote possibility that the infection may return is another reason not to drink.

LIVER CANCER RISK. Hepatitis-C-related liver damage increases your risk of liver cancer. Fortunately, eradication of the hepatitis C virus via DAA treatment lowers this risk. It does not, however, reduce the risk to that of someone without a history of hepatitis C. Alcohol use is one of the factors linked to the development of liver cancer after hepatitis C treatment.

I had to go on a course of injections for 12 months: Copegus in combination with Pegasys (peginterferon alfa-2a) and take pills every week. However, it was like having chemotherapy and I got extremely sick and was constantly vomiting. I also experienced extreme hair loss. Apparently, I am now clear of hepatitis C. Thank God for that small mercy.

The hepatitis C and the medication put a massive dent in our sex lives, and we didn't have intercourse for two years. Our sexual chemistry just wasn't there. I then did something that I will regret for the rest of my life. In 2014, I had an affair with a woman I'd met at one of my firewalking events, which lasted for around three months.

Mar-nelle cottoned on quite quickly that something was afoot and confronted me. I had to confess to the affair.

We spoke long and hard about it. I broke off the affair, and Mar-nelle and I tried for three years to make our relationship work. But I think this was a bridge too far for her and a slap in the face for her grace and the way she held us together through my many bad times.

In December 2017, she left with our children for Jeffreys Bay, never to return. The finality of her departure was still settling in when an unexpected ring at the door echoed through the empty spaces of our home. It was the estate security, accompanied by a man who introduced himself solemnly as the sheriff of the court. He was there to serve me divorce papers. The shock was palpable. I stood frozen, the papers in my hand a stark symbol of our dissolved vows.

Just moments after the papers were signed, the absence of Mar-nelle and the children filled the house with a profound silence. What followed was the loneliest period of my life—I spent Christmas and New Year's by myself, each festive chime a stark reminder of my isolation and the joy that used to fill those walls.

Those holidays, which were meant to be times of warmth and celebration, became a cold reflection of the solitude that had enveloped my life, marking the start of a new, but equally daunting, chapter.

I really couldn't blame her for leaving me. We were finally divorced in August 2019.

Besides the damage to the two of us, the damage to our two sons was huge. The fallout was heart-wrenching, as they initially turned against me—a reaction that, though painful, I understood given the circumstances. As a result, my interactions with them have become painfully infrequent, limited mostly to holidays. Despite this, I make concerted efforts to rebuild and strengthen our bonds.

Communication has been tough. They seldom initiate contact, and they aren't keen on using WhatsApp, which sometimes makes me feel disconnected and as though I'm missing out on significant portions of their lives. Even though there are obstacles, I believe that with time and effort, we could achieve forgiveness and reconciliation.

Whenever we do get the chance to be together, I emphasise creating new, joyful memories. These moments are precious and serve as building blocks for a slowly mending relationship. I never miss an opportunity to express my love and pride in them, showering them with hugs and kisses.

In 2014, I met Robin Banks. Little did I know what a major effect he would have on my life. We attended an event hosted by Success Resources Millionaire Mindset. I identified him as the guy from Mind Power. Do you recall John Kehoe? Robin took over from him in South Africa.

I approached him, handed him my business card, and told him to call me if he ever wanted to organise a firewalk. I knew that he did his first firewalking session with one of my mentors, Hannes Dreyer. I suspected that Robin wanted to be the Tony Robbins of South Africa, and that firewalking would appeal to him.

I saw marketing material for his Shape Your Destiny (SYD) event where he advertised a firewalking session, and I said to myself that I wanted to be the guy to do this event.

The day before the event, I got a phone call from Robin. Neil Malan, who was supposed to run the firewalking session, had to pull out and suggested that he call me. I was shocked and excited at the same time. I didn't want to appear too eager, so I told him that I needed to check my calendar.

A few minutes later, I called him and said I could do it. He then dropped the bombshell on me, saying he couldn't pay me and asking if I could do it for free. I agreed because his events had a large audience, which could help me gain fame as South Africa's firewalking expert.

However, I did require R25,000 to cover the cost of the firewalk and my expenses. I prayed and asked God to give me a sign that I was on the right path.

At the end of the event, a delegate came up and said he wanted to share something with the audience. He said that there's an inner voice telling him to give me some money. He reached into his pocket and gave me a bunch of rolled-up R200 notes. When I got home that afternoon, I counted the notes. The precise sum of money was R25 000. How miraculous was that? I definitely took it as a sign that I was on the right path.

I have since completed twelve more events for Robin, and I have been paid for all of them! I even did one for him in New Zealand. Robin witnessed first-hand the profound transformation in my life. He witnessed my transition from using a wheelchair to crutches and finally being able to walk again. Robin provided me not only with moral support but also with platforms to share my story.

I used to speak on his stages, where each appearance marked a significant milestone in my recovery and personal growth. Each time I spoke, the audience saw the progress I had made.

This visible journey not only inspired many but also deepened the bond and respect between Robin and me. His belief in my potential and his willingness to share his platform were crucial in helping me inspire others with my story.

I will forever be grateful that God put Robin on my path.

It was at the 2016 SYD event that I told everyone that I would be climbing Mount Kilimanjaro. At the time, I was using a wheelchair and crutches. They probably looked at me incredulously and thought that I was joking. My parents and friends certainly thought so.

In 2015, I watched a documentary about Bernard Goosen and Cameron Smith from South Africa. They both climbed Mount Kilimanjaro twice, even though they were in wheelchairs. Both were born with cerebral palsy. I thought that I probably wouldn't be able to do it in a wheelchair because my elbows would not bear it, but perhaps I could do it on crutches.

Everyone got really excited about this, and three people said that they would join me on the mountain. And they did: Chantal Kading, her brother, Jason van Schalkwyk, and Caz (Carrie-Ann) Mamotte.

Talking about climbing Mount Kilimanjaro is one thing; getting there is another thing.

It costs R60 000 - R80 000 to climb the mountain. Money I definitely did not have.

God sent me another sign. Chantal Kading returned her certificate of attendance with a note asking for my bank account information. On Monday morning, R25 000 was deposited into my bank account, which was exactly what I needed for my expenses. This felt like a sign from God, as I had been praying for one—hard. What an angel, what a miracle! I then knew that I would get to Mount Kilimanjaro.

Miraculously, another sign appeared, reaffirming the path that lay ahead of me. I met Will Butler at a firewalking event where my youngest son walked across fire for the first time. Our friendship quickly deepened, forged in the flames of that experience.

When Will told me he dreamt we would climb Mount Kilimanjaro together, I was surprised because I had secretly been wishing to conquer Mount Kilimanjaro myself, a dream I hadn't yet mentioned to anyone out loud. Hearing this from him felt like a nudge from the universe, a clear sign that this was more than mere coincidence.

I told Will about my ambition and that it felt like a sign from God that He was preparing me for this important journey. With Will's dream and my own goals aligning, they highlighted a strong connection and purpose, leading to a significant adventure in both our lives that wasn't just about climbing a mountain; it was about facing challenges and successes and moving forward with faith and friendship.

On this journey, an unexpected opportunity arose. Will asked me to coach him. Initially, I was taken aback by the request. Will, someone I saw as successful and accomplished, was seeking guidance from me. I was a coach who was dealing with a financial and deeply personal tornado at the time. The irony was not lost on me. Externally, I appeared to be stable and thriving, but in reality, I was residing with my parents and failing to meet my financial obligations.

The dichotomy between public perception and my private reality was stark. Despite this, Will's request was a beacon of potential. I decided to take on the role because I saw it as a chance to help a friend and also as a critical financial lifeline.

I agreed to coach him because I needed to, but also because I wanted to prove to myself that I could overcome my situation and help someone who believed in me.

This decision, though driven partly by financial necessity, became a significant part of my journey. It emphasised that our outward successes often hide inner battles and that helping others can motivate us to deal with our own labours.

After I coached him, I sent him an invoice. When he saw it, he said that it was way too cheap. He said, "Cobus, you are worth much more than that. Let me pay you what I think you're worth." He paid me R25 000. If that's not a sign, I don't know what is. Our coaching journey, which spanned from 2016 to 2020, turned out to be an evolution for the both of us. Under my guidance, Will's business flourished, growing from a modest R5 million to an astounding R100 million and more. Success wasn't just about money. Our relationship grew stronger, becoming a deep friendship based on respect and shared experiences.

Will often joked that I was not just his coach but also, inadvertently, responsible for the expansion of his family. After doing the firewalk, Will met Caz on the mountain and fell in love in such a powerful way that it culminated in the birth of their beautiful son.

My relationship with Will has been a testament to the power of faith and friendship. His role in my journey up Kilimanjaro was not merely that of a companion but of a guardian angel, embodying the divine presence that guided us to the summit. Through Will, I was reminded that true connections are forged through shared battles and triumphs, and that in those connections, we often find the face of God.

There are both affordable and luxurious options for climbing Mount Kilimanjaro. I required the luxurious choice. I needed an extra porter to carry my bags and my day pack. His name was Jackson, and he became my guardian angel.

I also needed a portable toilet at the camps because I wouldn't cope otherwise. For the Mount Kilimanjaro climb, I had to plan meticulously for my physical limitations, particularly considering my ankle condition. The standard facilities along the Machame Route were rudimentary at best, typically consisting of little more than a hole in the ground. This setup would be a predicament for anyone, but for someone with my specific mobility issues, it was unfeasible.

Given my inability to squat due to the condition of my ankles, it was essential to have a setup that allowed me to sit and stand with ease. Thus, bringing a portable toilet became vital for the journey. This addition was crucial not just for comfort but also for accessibility, ensuring that I could manage my needs independently without compromising my dignity or my safety.

Having the portable toilet allowed me to focus on the climb and the incredible experience of ascending Mount Kilimanjaro, rather than being preoccupied with the logistics that might have otherwise overshadowed this monumental task. I estimated that I needed anything north of R80 000 to make this happen.

I reached out to everyone, asking for their financial support. It was a humbling experience to make contact with friends and family for this kind of aid. Admitting the need for help stretched me, but the true heartbreak lay in the response—or lack thereof.

Surprisingly, many of those I considered close to me did not contribute, not even a modest R100. This silence from my immediate circle was disheartening and left me feeling isolated during a time when I expected understanding and support.

However, in the midst of this disappointment, the most unexpected generosity came from corners I had not anticipated. Individuals I had only met once or twice stepped forward to be there for me. Their unexpected kindness was not only a financial booster but also an emotional one. It reminded me that often, support comes from the most unexpected places, reinforcing the idea that the breadth of our impact on others can be vast and often unrecognised until moments like these.

This experience taught me valuable lessons about vulnerability.

I suppose, if I looked at me, I may not have bet on me either. Be that as it may, it still hurt that I didn't have the people I loved and cared for the most in my corner.

Then a miracle happened. In 2012, Mar-nelle and I went on a business trip to Tzaneen. Here we met André Ernst of Maluma Avocado, Allesbeste, the biggest avocado producer in Tzaneen.

In 2018, André saw a video I'd made regarding my Mount Kilimanjaro trip and reached out to me. He asked me how much the entire trip would cost. When I told him, he said his company would sponsor it in its entirety. I'm so sad that André passed away during the Covid pandemic and will not be able to read this book.

I wrote this letter to the Ernst family:

I HOPE THIS LETTER FINDS YOU enveloped in love during this difficult time. It is with a heavy heart filled with the most gratitude and respect that I write to you, reflecting on the incredible impact André had on my life.

Several years ago, your beloved André and I crossed paths in Tzaneen during a business trip related to my furniture enterprise. This chance meeting, seemingly ordinary at the time, grew into a pivotal connection that significantly altered the course of my life. André's warmth and genuine interest in the stories and dreams of others were immediately apparent, and it was this quality that later led to an act of generosity I could never have anticipated.

In 2018, after viewing a video I had sent out about my dream to climb Mount Kilimanjaro—a dream that seemed nearly impossible due to financial and physical constraints—André reached out with a heart so expansive that it still overwhelms me to think about it. Without hesitation, he offered to sponsor the entire journey through Maluma Avocado. This incredible gesture was not just a sponsorship but a lifeline that allowed me to fulfil a seemingly unreachable dream.

André's belief in my journey, which he shared with his son Zander, was nothing short of a blessing. It was as if providence had guided him to support me, and through his support, I was able to achieve something truly extraordinary. This experience profoundly impacted not only my life but also the lives of many others with whom I've shared my story, inspiring them to pursue their own dreams, regardless of the obstacles they face.

Sadly, the Covid-19 pandemic took away a remarkable man who was a pillar of strength, kindness, and generosity to all he encountered. André's passing is a tremendous loss, and I mourn with you, knowing that his presence will be dearly missed but also celebrated for the remarkable life he led.

Please know that André's spirit continues to inspire and motivate many, including myself. His legacy of kindness and his belief in the potential of others will continue to live on. I extend my deepest condolences to you, his cherished family. May you find some comfort in knowing how deeply he touched the lives of others and how greatly he is missed.

With all my respect and heartfelt sympathy,

COBUS

Knowing the impact Oom André had on enabling me to pursue my dreams, it's clear that his legacy extends far beyond the immediate gestures of support. His legacy is now intertwined with my journey and all that I do. This includes every chapter of this book, every talk I give, and every seminar I lead. Through these avenues, his spirit of generosity and belief in the potential of others continue to inspire and ignite passions.

His influence doesn't just live on in the memories of those who knew him or in the quiet acknowledgment of his kindness. Instead, it flourishes actively in the lives of those I reach through my work—lives he indirectly touched by setting me on my path. Every individual inspired by my story, every person who feels a little braver about pursuing their dreams, also echoes Oom André's faith and vision.

In this way, his legacy is dynamic and evolving, continuously impacting the world with positive waves that will reverberate for years to come. This profound and enduring effect is a testament to the kind of man he was, and it is my privilege and responsibility to ensure that his contribution is recognised and remembered. His support was a gift that fundamentally changed my life's course, and for that, I am eternally grateful.

By now, you know that I'm a haemophiliac who bounces around between wheelchairs and crutches. Climbing Mount Kilimanjaro is difficult enough for a fit and healthy person; it is near impossible for someone with haemophilia.

My doctor at the haemophilia clinics wouldn't support me and refused to sign my medical clearance certificate. He said that people die on the mountain. He said that I'm a haemophiliac (like I didn't know). He said that I could hardly walk and that my lungs would take a hit (he was right on that account).

Obviously, I went against both my doctor and family; otherwise, you wouldn't be reading this book now, would you?

I had friends who believed in me and would come to my house. They helped me to prepare every day. It was really hard at first. I remember that I could only walk to my front door and back in the beginning. Then I progressed to walking for an hour a day outside. I went on a five-kilometre hike at the Hennops Hiking Trail, then a few other trails in Faerie Glen and Groenkloof. For almost a week after that, I couldn't walk. But I continued to try. I got up and took my first steps, walking one step at a time, one step at a time. And, eventually, I could walk a fair distance.

Then I met Krupa Ratanjee. Krupa was truly an angel. She gave me 100% of her support during my Mount Kilimanjaro preparation and beyond that milestone. Her efforts went far beyond mere logistical support; she was the heart and soul behind the entire endeavour. From organising a heartfelt send-off party for me to managing the support networks on Facebook and WhatsApp, her dedication was a lighthouse of encouragement. She played a key role in getting community support and keeping everyone updated on the progress of the journey, making sure I never felt alone. Our relationship blossomed into a beautiful romance, and she became one of the best partners I have ever had. I will always love her, and I am deeply grateful for the role she played in my life.

Her enthusiasm was contagious, lifting the spirits of everyone involved, including mine. She was always there, supporting and celebrating my progress and comforting me during the tougher times. Krupa's presence made preparing for the mammoth task of climbing feel like a shared adventure with a community of supporters.

Calling her my biggest fan might sound cliché, but there's no other way to capture the essence of her unmoving faith in me. Her belief in me mirrored the belief I needed to have in myself, and for that, I am very grateful. Her role in this journey was pivotal, and her support is a testament to the power of having someone in your corner who believes in you unconditionally. Even after our relationship ended, Krupa's kindness and genuine concern for my well-being didn't falter. She regularly continued to check up on me, offering encouragement through various stages of my hurt. Her actions spoke volumes about her character—she is someone who cares deeply, not out of obligation but from a place of true compassion.

Having Krupa in my life during those times had been a lifeline for me on more than one occasion. Knowing that there was someone who cared, without any hidden agendas or malicious intent, had been incredibly reassuring.

She was constantly by my side, helping me prepare for my trip. We began as friends and then became a couple from September 2019 to October 2022. We are still good friends today.

She supported me through what was probably one of the most turbulent trials of my life. After my wife and sons left in December 2017, my world collapsed, and it took every inch of will to not fall down and die from a broken heart.

I fell straight into depression. I never left the house. I couldn't go anywhere. I just slept. I was stuck.

Krupa checked on me, but it must have been hard for her to deal with someone who was stagnating in feelings of pity and shame. But she stuck with me through everything. She really was something heavenly sent to me at a time I needed an angel the most.

At this time, an idea formed in my mind. A dirty secret that I never told anyone. Not Krupa; not anyone.

Initially, I decided to climb Mount Kilimanjaro to inspire both disabled and able-bodied people that they can achieve anything they aspire to. If I could climb Mount Kilimanjaro on crutches, what couldn't they do? I also wanted to show my sons that anything is possible.

When I read the news that celebrated South African rally driver Gugu Zulu had died while climbing Mount Kilimanjaro in 2016, my goal shifted.

I found a way out of this hell. I'd decided that I was going to kill myself on Mount Kilimanjaro. Or at least, I was going to let the mountain kill me. I was too much of a coward to take my own life.

In 2018, my mother helped me move out of my house and back to her's in Centurion. From then until July, I really started training for the mountain.

Preparing for Mount Kilimanjaro in 2018 was an ordeal that tested every ounce of my resilience. The journey to the summit was fraught not only with physical preparation but also with significant personal roadblocks that cast long shadows over my spirit.

Amidst the rigorous training required for something like this, I found myself grappling with depression. The solitude that often accompanies intensive preparation only deepens the loneliness. This period was also marked by the logistical stress of securing enough funds to cover all the expenses associated with the climb, adding financial pressure to an already emotionally taxing task.

To compound these difficulties, I was navigating the tumultuous waters of divorce proceedings. The emotional turmoil of dismantling a shared life, coupled with the ongoing legal complexities of divorce, was overwhelming. Pain was a constant companion.

As the date of the climb drew nearer, the convergence of these obstacles became increasingly daunting. The weight of my circumstances made the mountain ahead seem even steeper. Yet, through this crucible of preparation, I was forging a new level of tenacity and determination. Each day brought me closer not only to Mount Kilimanjaro but also to a deeper understanding of my own strengths and capabilities. The path was undeniably tough, but it was also an expedition that taught me about the surprising elasticity of the human spirit when faced with seemingly insurmountable odds.

Farewell: 6 July

Everyone is getting ready to climb Mount Kilimanjaro, and we share a goodbye at the clubhouse at Centurion Golf Estate, where my parents live. The entire family is there to wish me well, even my sons.

I'm excited and nervous. What am I thinking, climbing Africa's highest mountain with crutches? But what does it matter? I'm going there to die anyway. This is where I end my pain.

For me, this is a bittersweet moment. I'm convinced it will be the last time I see all my loved ones.

My parents and my sons have dinner together at Wimpy fast food in OR Tambo International Airport. Soon, it is time for me to meet the other six climbers on our team at the boarding gate. Carrie-Ann (Caz) Mamotte would only arrive the next day and had to travel alone. There are lots of tears, hugs, and love as we say goodbye.

I also feel remorse because they think I'm coming back from Mount Kilimanjaro. I don't intend to, that's for sure.

The team boarded the plane. We're heading to Kenya and taking the connecting flight to Tanzania. We strap in and wait for take-off to embark on the biggest adventure of our lives. We're all silent, lost in our own thoughts. We're processing our hopes, dreams, and fears.

The team was comprised of Taryn-lee Kearney, brother and sister Chantal Kading and Jason van Schalkwyk, Will Butler, Andrea Bogner, Tanya du Toit, and me.

Four hours later, our plane lands at Nairobi Airport, Kenya. We hop onto the connecting flight to Mount Kilimanjaro Airport, Tanzania.

We fly past Mount Kilimanjaro. It's massive, foreboding, and intimidating. It's breath-taking. It's beautiful. I cannot believe that I'm going to try to summit this colossus. From above, it looks like an impossible task.

When we land, we are met by our guides and the owner of the company that has been tasked with caring for us. They greet us with warm smiles and introduce themselves, eager to embark on this adventure together.

They explain the plan for the next week, filling us with excitement for what's to come.

I wake up with anticipation. I've brought my medicine with me. Without which, I won't make it. I inject 2000 units of plasma and head off for breakfast.

Facing the rigorous conditions of a mountain climb with a medical condition adds a significant layer of complexity to the adventure. Managing medical needs, such as plasma injections, in a harsh environment like a mountainside is daunting. The daily regimen of injecting 6 000 units of medication each morning ensures that your factor levels remain high enough to withstand the physical demands of climbing, reducing the risk of bleeding into the joints.

We leave the hotel at 08h00. It's a two-hour drive to the base of the mountain.

We arrive at the gates to the entrance of Mount Kilimanjaro. It looks like something off the set of Jurassic Park. Tall and imposing, the gates beckon us to step into a prehistoric wonderland. The anticipation builds as we pass through them, wondering what lies beyond.

At the gate of Mount Kilimanjaro, one of the first official tasks is to sign the register. This procedure is crucial for both safety and accountability. It ensures that every climber who ascends the mountain is documented and accounted for, which is vital for organising rescue efforts if needed and ensuring all climbers return safely.

Signing the register is more than a mere formality; it represents a commitment to the journey ahead and a reminder of the mountain's gauntlet. It also serves as a check-in point, a way for authorities to keep track of who is on the mountain at any given time, enhancing the safety of everyone involved.

This process underscored the importance of responsibility and preparedness as we embarked on this formidable adventure. It's a moment of pause, where the magnitude of the undertaking sinks in—every name in the register carries a story of aspiration and courage, and mine joins the chorus of those seeking to conquer not just Mount Kilimanjaro but personal limitations.

There's a lot of excited chatter as we wait to start the adventure of our lives. We take photos while anticipating the climb. It starts raining. It sends a chill up my spine because I see the rain as a harbinger of things to come. It suddenly hits me that this is not going to be easy, by any stretch of the imagination.

At 12h00, we're still waiting. We're all like tensed-up racehorses, champing at the bit to get going. I'm already exhausted from all the waiting. But when the guides indicate that it's time to leave, the exhaustion fades into the background, replaced by a renewed sense of excitement.

We have a seven-hour journey ahead of us before we rest for the day. I'm amazed at the fitness and strength of the porters who race ahead of us to set up camp. They're carrying a lot of equipment.

Our Swahili guides keep reminding us to pole pole (pronounced po-lay)—to walk slowly, slowly. We need to conserve our energy. An hour in, and I'm already feeling the effects. My crutches chafe me under the arms.

We're in a rain forest, so it's extremely slippery. It takes all my concentration not to fall. I can hardly breathe. It feels like my lungs are filling up with water. I get this weird cough and feel cold. Taking deep breaths is laborious. I feel like I'm getting sick; my joints are burning with pain.

We ask our guide how far it is to the next camp. He said that the moment you smell popcorn, you're close. I think he's joking. But it's true. Because one typically gets to a camp in the dark, the smell of popcorn acts as a guide to the destination.

Eventually, we smelled the popcorn; what a relief! It's almost 20h00 and pitch black. There's no power. It's muddy. My tent is full of mud. I'm full of mud. My bag was in the tent, and the air mattress was laid out. The sight was incredibly inviting. I just wanted to lie on it and go to sleep. But I had to eat. I left my crutches in the tent and crawled to where the food was being served, and it was delicious.

With our bellies full and a warm fire thawing us out, we started talking amongst ourselves.

I decided to come clean with my group and told them that I wasn't coming off the mountain. That this would be my last journey. That I'm here to die. They laughed it off and said that I wouldn't die here. My friend Will Butler said, "You're not going to die; I'll make sure you come back with us."

Summary of Audio Recordings: End of Day 1

In preparation for tomorrow, I grab some tissues as well as all my jackets—it seems I still have a whole pack of tissues in my pocket from earlier. I've yet to change my pants, maintaining a rugged readiness for whatever comes our way.

Will Butler: *Today brought its share of weightless moments. While giving my back a break, my contact lens popped out, surprisingly still wet, which allowed me to quickly remedy the situation. A moment like this might've been an inconvenience on another day; today, it is somewhat humorous.*

As we wrap up the day, others reminisce about past climbs, the durability of our gear, and the potential for meaningful connections to form within our group. We talk seriously for a while, then drift back to blithe banter.

Looking ahead to tomorrow, we are reminded not to rush. Our pace is determined not just by the physical trail but also by the strength and spirit of our group. Today was just the beginning, and as we continue, each step will bring us closer not only to our destination but to each other.

Thank you all for a remarkable first day. Here's to tomorrow— may it bring us closer to our goals. Let's continue to support one another, share in the beauty of our surroundings, and enjoy every moment of this incredible journey.

We all sign off.

Today we trekked through the lush rainforest, a vibrant ecosystem alive with the calls of hidden creatures and the rustle of leaves. Tomorrow promises a stark contrast as we transition into the moorland or heather zone. It's a shorter journey, expected to last about five hours. We plan to start at seven in the morning and aim to reach the camp by noon for a well-deserved lunch. After refuelling, we'll have some time to relax and maybe take a brief walk around the camp if the weather permits, before returning for dinner and sleep.

Chief guide, Nelson: *Tomorrow's terrain will be quite demanding, mostly uphill. The path ahead is steep, and we'll be ascending most of the day, navigating slippery rocks at a slow pace to ensure everyone's safety. It's important to continue our 'pole pole' (slowly, slowly) approach to conserve our energy and adjust to the altitude.*

Our gear strategy for tomorrow is simple but essential. The morning won't be very cold since we'll still be below the cloud line. However, as we ascend and potentially move above the clouds by the afternoon, temperatures can drop. I recommend wearing long pants and packing a light fleece in your daypack. Adding a long-sleeved layer to your outfit can help you adjust to changing conditions throughout the day.

In terms of logistics, we'll start our day early. At around 06h00, someone will pass by your tents to say good morning and bring hot water for coffee or tea, setting a comforting start to the day. Make sure your larger bags are packed before you head to breakfast because, by the time we're eating, the support team will begin to break down the tents.

For breakfast, expect a hearty meal to fuel the strenuous day ahead. We're talking bread, toast, pancakes, and porridge—enough to keep you energised for hours. After breakfast, we'll engage in a bit of a social icebreaker, introducing everyone to foster a sense of togetherness. We might even dance a little to lift our spirits before we commence the day's hike.

I can't stress enough the importance of supporting each other throughout this journey. The path we're on is as much about the physical as it is about building bonds and helping one another through the tough spots. Remember, this expedition is not just about reaching the peaks; it's about the shared experiences and the growth we achieve together.

Lastly, a reminder about hydration and meal requests: don't hesitate to ask for what you need, be it more water or a specific dietary requirement. The phrase 'Naomba chakula, tafadhali' can be your friend here—it means, "May I have some food, please?" in Swahili.

Thank you all for your hard work and positive attitudes today. Let's carry this energy forward as we face the uphills of tomorrow. Looking forward to another day of adventure and teamwork as we continue our ascent.

Day 1: Reflections and Insights

Tonight, as we settle down from the day's journey, I will continue to share insights and teachings, hoping to provide guidance and inspiration as we prepare for tomorrow's tests.

Thank you, everyone. Your endurance today was remarkable, and your spirits were high, even though I know many of you are feeling the strain. Before we retire for the evening, I'd like to take a moment to acknowledge a few individuals who exemplified extraordinary resilience and leadership today.

Firstly, Jason, you've been a rock star throughout this journey—your strength and spirit have been nothing short of inspiring. And Taryn-lee, you're not far behind. Success isn't just about reaching the heights; it's about the journey you take to get there. It's about where you started and the hurdles you've overcome along the way. Today, you didn't just keep pace; you closed gaps, proving that true victory lies in the courage to continue.

CHANTAL KADING: *This morning's rush for lunch at the main camp brought the realisation that each of us carries an invisible provision. Behind every one of us is a network of friends, family, mentors, and sponsors who've helped us reach this point. Our individual efforts on Uhuru Peak will be the culmination of collective encouragement and support. Remember, no one achieves greatness in isolation. If you face a challenge, reach out. Help is always available, and often all it takes is asking.*

As we venture forward, be mindful of the community we're creating. The strength we derive from each other here will resonate beyond this mountain. Tomorrow's climb will be tough, but as a unit, we are tougher. Let's carry today's lessons forward, supporting, learning, and growing together.

Now, as we prepare for tomorrow, ensure your gear is ready and your spirits are high. We start early, so I'll be around to make sure everyone gets a warm wake-up call. Remember, a hearty breakfast awaits, providing the fuel we'll need to go higher. Dress appropriately; the terrain will be challenging, but our preparation today ensures our success tomorrow.

WILL BUTLER: *When asked about my nerves concerning the mountain, my response was resolute: I welcomed it. Some may find this attitude perplexing, likening me to a madman, but there's a profound reason behind it. I've always seen the mountain as a place where I might rediscover something lost or uncover something new about myself.*

The physical aspect of this climb, while demanding, isn't my primary focus. My true goal is to ensure that everyone reaches the summit. This collective success means more to me than my own.

Today, Taryn-lee, you've particularly impressed me with your resilience. You've shown great strength, maybe even more than you realise, reminding us of the personal victories that come with our physical achievements.

In boxing, the toughest rounds are known as the championship rounds. These are the moments when you want to quit, but you keep going. That's exactly what today represented. Each step you took, Taryn-lee, was a testament to your tenacity. You've taught us all a valuable lesson in perseverance, and for that, I thank you sincerely.

As we move ahead, let's remember that we have a whole network of people back home supporting our journey. Each step we take is bolstered by their faith in us. This climb is symbolic of any life challenge, and just like today, reaching out for support can make all the difference.

Let's continue to leverage our collective strengths, sharing our burdens and our skills. Our diversity is our greatest asset, allowing us to support each other where it counts the most. My hope is that as we move forward, each of us will continue to learn—not just about the mountain but about ourselves and each other.

Thank you all for a fantastic day. Let's rest well tonight; tomorrow will always bring something new, but we'll face it together. One step at a time.

In reflection, I'm reminded that it's not solely about reaching the summit. Climbing a mountain like this is fundamentally a journey of three dimensions: the physical, the emotional, and the spiritual. It's crucial to acknowledge that sometimes, despite our best efforts, reaching the top may not be possible. This realisation is not an admission of defeat but a testament to our self-awareness and the maturity to acknowledge our limits.

If we can achieve 90 percent of our goal, why not push for 95 percent? Yet, in doing so, we must remain truthful with ourselves. It's vital to recognise when to advance and when to retreat, always prioritising well-being over ambition. The real triumph lies not at the peak but in the lessons learned with each step we take.

In the early hours today, as I penned thoughts in my journal—a habit I've maintained for inspiration—I revisited a concept from a book I read three years ago. It spoke about the necessity to shed the emotional shackles, mental roadblocks, and physical excuses that often hold us back. This climb, this formidable challenge of Mount Kilimanjaro, embodies that very message. Over the next week, we'll each confront these barriers in various forms, and I hope we all find the strength to overcome them.

As we gather for dinner tonight, let's celebrate the progress we've made, not just towards the mountain's summit, but within ourselves. Here's to the meals that replenish us, the conversations that enrich us, and the communal spirit that sustains us. Let's savour this moment and continue to support each other on this incredible journey.

Thank you all for being here, for the efforts you've put in, and for the companionship that's blossomed among us. Let's enjoy our dinner and prepare for what lies ahead. We're in this together.

Goodnight, everyone, and see you in the morning.

By the time our guide came to wake me up, I was already up. I'd set my alarm for an hour earlier than everyone else. I have to inject myself with plasma every morning, and it takes me at least half an hour to get out of my sleeping bag and get dressed. For me, dressing is not so simple. Every morning I have to put on ankle, knee, and elbow guards to protect me. I also had to pack my snacks, power banks, and Go-Pro camera into my backpack.

My guide gives me a cup of hot ginger tea. I gulp it down with gusto. It warms me up beautifully.

As we all gathered for the journey, the porters sang this song:

Jambo, jambo Bwana

(Hello, hello Sir)

Habari gani

(How are you?)

Mzuri sana

(Very fine)

Wageni, mwakaribishwa

(Foreigners, you're welcome)

Kenya yetu, hakuna matata

(Our Kenya has no problems)

Kenya nchi nzuri, hakuna matata

(Kenya is a nice country; there are no problems)

Nchi ya maajabu, hakuna matata

(Country of wonders, there are no problems)

Nchi yenye amani, hakuna matata

(Country of peace, there are no problems)

Watu wote, hakuna matata

(Everybody, there are no problems)

Wakaribishwa, hakuna matata

(All are welcome; there are no problems)

Hakuna matata, hakuna matata

(There are no problems, there are no problems)

There's only five days to go. But I'm in pain, I'm tired, and I'm miserable. I'm ready to give up. I know that this leg of the journey is two hours shorter than the first one. So, I trick my mind by saying that the journey will be shorter. I decided to push on and make a call at the next camp. Little did I know how harrowing the next leg would be.

We finally break through the rain forest to be confronted by an imposing rock face. Climbing up the rocks was daunting because the danger of slipping and falling was very real. It took a lot of concentration and focus not to fall. A number of people in our group did slip and fall. Luckily, nobody was hurt.

Because I don't have ankles, I have to concentrate twice as hard as the others. One fall can spell disaster for me. I had to climb the entire way using the front of my feet and my toes. Every night when I rested, the thing that hurt the most were my calves. Every night, they cramped.

I grappled on Day 2. It was then that I started praying. I prayed every step of the way that God would guide my feet so that I wouldn't fall. Of course, the irony is not lost on me: I wanted to live, even though I came to die.

Finally, we break through the clouds, and the sun is out. It's not wet anymore; it's dry.

I see the clouds below me. It feels like I broke through them and into heaven. I remember having a snack and thinking how beautiful it all was. I was grateful to be able to witness the surrounding beauty.

We carry on walking along a path. And then terror rears its head. There is a gap in the path, and if you look left, there's a void. One wrong move, and you fall to your death.

We have to jump from one ledge to the next. I can't do it because of my ankles and crutches. But I need to jump, or this journey is over for me. I tell my guides that I can't do it. Just the thought of jumping and landing on my ankles was too much for me to take in.

They encourage me and say that I can do this. They tie a rope to me. It gives me a sense of safety. I'm scared. It feels like it takes me forever to jump; I am terrified. This is the biggest jump of my life. But I jumped, and I'm so glad that I did. A guide on the other side of the ledge catches me. I almost cry with relief. The second jump is easier, as I know I can make it.

It is now that I realise that I can't go back to the base camp because I will have to jump back the way I came. That's okay because I don't plan on coming down the mountain anyway.

We finally reach our camp, which is on a wide ledge. It is *beautiful.* You can see the clouds at the bottom. I get to my tent and collapse. A guide comes in and says that we need to go on a two-hour hike so that we can acclimatise. It's not a compulsory hike. But the goal is to help one adapt so that they can get used to the altitude. I decided not to hike. I can't. I am in such pain. The choice to stay had a massive impact on me when we summitted. I'll speak of that later.

We later sat around the gas fire, enjoying a beautiful dinner and sharing our experiences. That was the first night that we saw stars. For me, it was the most beautiful sight in the world.

Day 2: Audio Shares

Day 2 commenced with liveliness as we regrouped after a night of restful (and, for some, sonorous) sleep. There was a lot of snoring going on last night.

Day 2 unfolded as a serene testament to reflection and connection, marked by personal revelations on the mountain. As the evening ended, we moved from thinking on our own to a group area called 'The Smoke Club,' where people could stay or go to bed.

Today, I found myself in a contemplative state, reflecting on the sage advice once given by my grandfather. He told me to never return from a journey the same way I went. This puzzled me in my youth, but today I grasp its profound meaning. We often travel through life on autopilot, retracing the same paths without awareness. Today, I consciously broke that cycle. I took my time, appreciated the calmness, and observed the world around me. I used my camera to capture moments and enjoyed the peacefulness.

I took this pause to remember important people who have influenced my life, such as my grandfather and uncle. The day was calm and peaceful, giving us a chance to appreciate our surroundings and think about the people who have had a profound impact on our lives.

The journey through the hills today was unexpectedly invigorating. Charles, our chief guide, reassured us that each hill was just another small step. However, his assurances did not prepare us for the reality of six further ascents. Yet, each peak brought a new level of exhilaration. Seeing the clouds from above for the first time was an amazing experience that made me feel closer to God.

The physical demands of the day were tiring, but they didn't take away from the joy of just being present. The personal victories of overcoming each hill resonated deeply with me, reinforcing the belief that we are all capable of surpassing our perceived limits.

The day unfolded with an easier rhythm. The pace, more accessible. The day was marked not just by physical trekking but by mental and spiritual journeys as well. I found solace in the epic, wordless music that resonated with scenes from movies like 'Gladiator' and 'Braveheart,' which accompanied me through the day's hike, stirring deep emotional responses.

Today's journey through the landscape was a poignant reminder of my grandfather's wisdom—never to return the same way. This became a metaphor for life, urging me not to fall into monotony but to embrace each moment anew. This approach changed today into a series of mindful moments where I consciously avoided autopilot, fully engaging with the environment and the companionship of my fellow climbers.

Physically, this was a Herculean task, with precarious rocks threatening stability, yet the support within the group, particularly from Taryn-lee and Will, provided strength and motivation.

As we ascended above the clouds, the surreal beauty of our surroundings was a vivid reminder of the divine craftsmanship of nature—breath-taking, humbling.

The terrain shifted under our feet, moving what was expected to be a hike into segments of rigorous rock climbing. These physical tests were met with resilience, as every member of our group found their strength tested yet buoyed by the collective spirit.

Today, we talked. From a heart space. The solidarity within the group was palpable, with each member contributing invaluable encouragement for other climbers.

As the day concluded, the sentiment of gratitude was universal. We were not just climbing a mountain; we were learning about resilience, about the power of community, and about the profound impact of nature on our spirits. Techniques were shared on how to ground and deeply connect with the earth for our physical and mental well-being. Nature always provides.

During the evening, music played an important role, with songs divinely aligning with the motivation we needed as we looked ahead towards the summit. The song 'World's Greatest' perfectly captured the essence of our adventure.

The adventure, it seems, was also in uncovering who the people we walked with were at their core. Off the mountain, they were coaches, human resource recruiters, integrative therapeutic technique practitioners, adventure capitalists. Whatever the calling was off the mountain, it brought each of us to a pinnacle point in the discovery of our purpose, each making them strong and driven enough to make this climb.

The food we ate every day was a celebration of the local cuisine and was intentionally made and served by mindful people walking the path with us. We thanked every one of them for sustaining us and immersing us in a rich cultural experience.

The value of being surrounded by a diversity of highly driven people is uncovering what fuels them to be great. One shared principle was being present in every moment and exercising gratitude. This is how we can embrace the 'power of now'. Another sentiment is that every person inherently possesses goodness, despite sometimes making poor choices. Seek the goodness in others, and goodness you will find.

We were quickly brought back to mentally gearing for the day ahead—with expected shifts in temperature and terrain, we were encouraged to keep our rain gear handy, preparing for an early start to ensure that we have enough time to reach our destination without rushing.

In order to subvert the potential of Acute Mountain Sickness (AMS), a part of our preparation was to have lunch at a higher altitude before descending to a lower altitude to sleep, aiding in better acclimatisation. To also start prepping as early as we possibly could.

5 .a.m. club, here we come.

DAY 3: 11 JULY

The next morning, I wake up once again an hour earlier than anyone else because of my routine. The hot beverages the porter brought me were heaven-sent.

At breakfast, we were served bacon. I tasted it, and it just didn't taste right. It didn't smell right either. Stupidly, I ate two pieces before stopping. The dire ramifications came later.

Today, we packed light. I'm feeling good; my body is playing along nicely. This is going to be a good day, I think.

We are on our way to our next stop, the Lava Tower Camp, which is 4 600 m above sea level.

A Lava Tower is an ancient formation that is believed to be the result of a volcanic vent. It appears to have occurred when molten lava emerged from a vent in the ground and then cooled and hardened, eventually blocking up the vent and leaving behind a steep, tower-like structure.

Our guide tells us that there is no toilet at Lava Tower Camp and that we'll have to use the 'hole in the ground'—a shed with a literal hole in the ground. A stinky one at that.

As we start, the environment changes. As far as the eye can see, there are grey rocks stretching out everywhere. There are rock towers built by previous climbers all around us.

In this environment, there's no place to hide. Neither a tree nor a blade of grass are in sight. Just grey rocks. I imagine that this must be what it's like to be on the moon.

The little voice in my head is saying, "You can't do this, Cobus. Why don't you just give up? You're going to give it all up soon, anyway. Save yourself the pain and give up now. Go and die."

Well, there was no way I was going to die before I summited Uhuru Peak. So, I drowned out the voices and focused on the surrounding beauty. It's an eight-hour trek, and if I don't find something to focus on, I'll be in trouble.

All that I see are grey rocks. But when I focus, I find beautiful flowers among them. It occurs to me that there is beauty in every situation; you just have to look for it.

I rest a lot because of my ankles. The crutches tire me. The group is already way ahead of me. Suddenly, my stomach cramps. Damn you, bacon. I feel like I'm going to explode. I ask the guide how far it is to the Lava Tower. He said that I should look up. I see the Lava Tower; we're not far anymore.

Even though it's a short distance, it looks like an unending road. I'm not sure I'm going to make it to the hole in the ground.

I'm shivering and sweating. By sheer force of will (by holding my knees together and loosening my belt), I manage to stagger into camp.

I remember that I have to use a hole, which would be a problem for me even on a normal day. But with diarrhoea, it will be a complete disaster.

And then a miracle. I see that the guides have put up a portable toilet after all. I thank God and waddle my way to the toilet. What a relief!

The diarrhoea has taken its toll. I'm feeling extremely weak, and I can't eat the lunch that was served. I consume energy drinks, water, and valoids (for nausea) to keep myself energised and hydrated.

After lunch, we head off again for a five-hour journey to our next camp, Barranco. It was the longest and most gruelling five hours of my life. My knees and ankles are in constant pain. For every 10 steps I take, I rest for a couple of minutes. It's as if it will never end.

I find the will to carry on. Prayer and grit are all I have now. And, of course, my angel, Jackson, the porter who carries my backpack. His words of encouragement bolster my flagging spirits.

Walk. Rest. Walk. Rest. Walk. Rest. I smell popcorn. I'm almost there. Slowly, slowly. Pole pole. I'm almost there.

My teammates have been there for a while. After I freshen up in my tent, I join them for dinner. I love dinner time. It's where we get to share. And, best of all, I am building a beautiful friendship with everyone around me.

Remember, this is me, Jason, Chantal, Taryn-lee, Andrea, Tanya, Caz, and Will. Jason and Chantal are siblings, and they're like my family. They both looked after me. Chantal, in particular, was a pillar of support throughout the climb. She'd be there with energy bars and water, making sure that I was cared for.

The rest of the group naturally paired up and encouraged each other: Andrea and Tanya; Chantal and Jason; Caz and Will; me and Jackson; Taryn-lee and her guide.

Jason and Chantal pushed themselves hard. But they always paused and made sure that I got my energy bars and water before they moved on. Andrea and Tanya became friends. Andrea became the Iron Lady, helping Tanya push through a daunting time on the mountain.

Andrea and Tanya always got to the next camp first. Jason and Chantal second. Caz and Will, our two lovebirds, came in third. Taryn-lee and I were consistently the ones bringing up the rear.

Tanya started a meaningful conversation by comparing the changing landscapes of mountains to the different stages of life, highlighting the importance of each phase and the growth or healing it brings.

This resonates with Jason, who reflected on the importance of appreciating moments rather than mourning their passing. He highlighted the transformative power of shifting focus from what is lost to the beauty and opportunities that lie ahead.

The group also acknowledged the substantial support from the trekking team, recognising the effort of the 31 people working diligently to help them achieve their goal. This acknowledgement brought a sense of humility and gratitude, reinforcing the message that no significant achievement is ever a solo effort but rather a collective endeavour requiring support and teamwork.

WILL BUTLER: *Okay, thank you for waiting, Nelson. Yes, so when we descended from Lava Tower, it was daunting. The decline was steep, and the rocks were slippery, which really put our bodies to the test. I realised then how crucial it was to have support. Every step was a mix of pain and prayer, but also profound gratitude. The team—Jackson, Alex, and Dixon— were my pillars today, constantly reassuring and aiding me. Their dedication was a powerful reminder of the importance of community and support in overcoming life's mountains.*

As we trudged towards Barranco Camp, I couldn't help but think about the things I've faced in my own life. Being a haemophiliac has always meant dealing with physical limits, but today, more than ever, I felt those boundaries push back against me. Yet, instead of fighting alone, I was surrounded by people who were literally and figuratively supporting me every step of the way.

This journey is difficult. There were moments today where I felt overwhelmed by the support—these people, who hardly know me, were there to ensure I made it. It makes you think about the kind of support we all deserve but often don't receive. How many times have we had to face our conflict alone because we were too proud or too afraid to ask for help?

Today was a testament to the power of letting others in and allowing them to help us climb our mountains. It was also a reminder that no matter how strong or independent we think we are, everyone benefits from a supportive community.

So, as we sit here tonight, I just want to express my deepest gratitude to everyone here. To the team who's been with us every step of the way, to my fellow climbers who've shared their stories and strength, and to the serene, rugged beauty of this mountain that continues to teach us about ourselves. Thank you, all of you, for being part of my journey.

Alright, that's very reassuring, thank you. It's crucial that everyone feels safe and supported, especially in trickier sections like the kissing rock. This is when the collective effort of the group and the expertise of our guides really shine through. It's comforting to know that you have measures in place for everyone's safety and comfort.

I appreciate the additional porter support as well. That will certainly help those who might struggle with the physical demands of carrying a daypack while navigating the terrain. It's these thoughtful considerations that make a significant *difference in our experience and ability to focus on the journey itself.*

CHIEF GUIDE, NELSON: *If no one has any further questions or concerns, I think we're ready to wrap up for tonight. Tomorrow sounds like it will be an exciting day with beautiful views. Let's get a good rest tonight, so we're all energised and ready to tackle the Barranco Wall. Thank you again for the briefing and the continuous support. Let's keep up the great teamwork and push on towards our goal together.*

Goodnight, everyone.

I awoke to the sounds of a helicopter landing. This meant that it was here to pick someone up. Altitude sickness was a common reason for helicopters to come by. It wasn't just our group in the camp, but others too.

This is the last place a helicopter can safely land. My little voice is saying, "Come on, Cobus, pack it up. There's no shame in it. Quit now."

I shush my voice. There's no way I'm not summiting Uhuru.

We're spending more and more time in spaces that wouldn't have a trace of a cell phone signal, but I managed to call Krupa. I was very emotional. When I put the phone down, I just sobbed. Through my tears, I look up at our next climb, a mountain called Barranco Wall.

I stop crying and focus on centring myself. This is going to be a tough one. The doubts creep in.

As a haemophiliac, I don't have elbows. With significant to complete cartilage deterioration, how am I going to push my body up by myself? It's not just a normal hike to the top. There are places that require you to pull yourself up. I can't. No, I can't. I go to the chief guide and tell him that I can't do this. He calms me down and says that I shouldn't worry. He's going to assign me an additional porter to assist Jackson. One will be in front and one behind to make sure that I don't fall.

I am calm, and I accept that I'll go on. I have come here to die, after all. If God decides it'll be on Barranco Wall, so be it.

I get dressed and put my face mask on. As I look up, I see Jason cry. He's afraid of heights. I can't believe that there's someone just as scared as I am. I recognise what he's going through, but I can't help him; I can only love him. This is his journey. I have to conquer my own journey. I can only help myself so that I can live (for as short as I plan it to be) without regret.

I have to do this. Here we go. I can do it. We start to climb. Other climbers pass me, and I stand close to the wall so that they can come by.

Climbing Barranco Wall tested my trust and taught me that sometimes you just need to let go and let someone else take over. I had to put my life in the hands of two porters that I barely knew. Just a few days before, two porters fell to their deaths. "You're in it now, Cobus," I thought. "You just have to trust."

One part of the climb was extreme. It's called Kissing Rock. You have to go from one rock to the next by stretching out your arms. You actually have to kiss the rock, or you go over the ledge and fall to your death.

There is one porter who continuously referred to me as Mufasa—the lion. As time has gone by, his name has slipped my mind, so from here on we will call him Mufasa.

Mufasa and Jackson must have possessed extraordinary strength to support me. I weighed 120 kilogrammes at the time. In the places we had to climb, one porter would pull me up, and the other would push me up. They did this with equanimity and with such love. My angels, they were. Without them, I never would have made it.

I can't believe it. I'm doing this. It becomes more difficult as we ascend, yet with this climb, I never once look down. Eventually, I get to the top. The rest of the team, as per usual, were there before me. There were hugs all round, and snacks were doled out. We were all tired, but we were satisfied and proud because we had achieved something significant.

But then reality kicked in. We were only 25% of the way to our next camp. We still had three quarters to go.

It turned hot and humid. I was drenched with sweat 100 metres into the next leg of our journey. The terrain was like a desert. There were dunes, and we were to climb two steps up and slide one step down. Excruciating.

The sun was getting to me. Even though I had applied copious amounts of sunscreen, I could feel my face ablaze. I knew I'd have a bad case of sunburn.

The sand almost kills me, as it saps every ounce of energy I have left. Once again, everyone is ahead of me. It's just me and Jackson.

I take two steps and then breathe. I take two minutes to get my breath back, and so it goes. It takes me hours to get to the top. I have to talk to myself to stop thinking about the pain and the fear.

My mind suddenly starts spinning. There are no voices. How's this possible? It is dead quiet in my head. I only have my physical voice to count on. I have to talk to myself and motivate myself to keep moving. It is a surreal experience. And by the time I get to the top, I sound like a rambling lunatic.

I finally make it to my tent and collapse with exhaustion. I've hardly got time to catch my breath when dinner is called, just before sunset.

I need to go to the toilet before heading off to dinner, and I'm so glad that I do.

It is the most spectacular view I've ever seen from anywhere else in the world, let alone a toilet. These lavatories are set up in such a way that one has a full view down from above the clouds. There are no words to describe how surreal it is.

As I sit beside my teammates at dinner, I have time to really think. I don't think any one of us realised what we were getting ourselves into. None of us were climbers. Andrea is probably the fittest because she goes to the gym regularly. Jason is a sports addict. Will, who runs marathons, grapples with asthma. I can see that Chantal is feeling it.

Taryn-lee is struggling as much as I am. Taryn-lee and I bonded through our shared suffering. Yet that night, I felt so alone. That night, I prayed like never before. "God, please save me because I'm on my way to die. This is my last journey. This is my last chapter. I don't want to go back. I'm a failure. I couldn't even be a dad. I'm a coward. My business is on the verge of collapse. My dad is not speaking to me. Nobody loves me. I have nothing to go back to. Please give me peace."

After praying, something almost divine happened. Karanga Camp is 3 900 metres above sea level and was the closest I'd ever been to the moon and the stars. I looked up, and it felt like I could reach out, touch them, and pull them down. At that moment, my heart was filled with awe and such deep gratitude.

The climb is gruelling, but everyone is moving with a profound togetherness.

The crew makes sure everyone is well-fed and energised, adapting meals to keep everyone's spirits and energy up. As Malcolm Forbes once said, "Food may be essential as fuel for the body, but good food is fuel for the soul."

The climbers are nervous and excited, but the team ensures that they we always prepared. We're encouraged to pool our resources—snacks, gels, energy bars. We help balance our supplies to make sure everyone is taken care of if the need arises.

This strategy also encourages everyone to communicate their needs and contributions transparently, reinforcing trust and interdependence. Sharing resources this way ensures that no one is left without essential supplies, which is crucial for safety and success on such a demanding adventure. It's a testament to the saying, "We're only as strong as our weakest link," reminding everyone that looking out for each other is paramount.

WILL BUTLER: *Yes, Gibson. Gibson, can you come here for a moment, please?*

Thank you.

Just to add to what Nelson was saying, I think it's crucial to ensure we're all prepared mentally and physically for what lies ahead. The gradual climb, the proper hydration, and the right gear are essential, but equally, our mental readiness is vital.

Under the starts, we anticipate tomorrow's climb with a mix of excitement and apprehension. Nelson prays, and the plans for the summit attempt highlight all of our reliance on both spiritual support and meticulous planning. The challenge of the climb is clear, but so is our determination. We find solace in that.

Like every morning, I wake up an hour earlier. Only one more day to go before we summit.

I get dressed. I inject myself. I make sure to recharge my electronic devices. I'm raring to go and eat breakfast. They say today is a short walk because we are going to the base camp at Uhuru Peak. It takes us five hours to get to the camp.

We are told to rest because we will be heading out again at 21h00 and 23h00. Taryn-lee and I would move out at 21h00 because we are the slowest. This means that if the rest of the team leaves at 23h00, they'd catch us at some stage, and hopefully we'd all reach our destination at the same time.

I try to sleep in my tent, but it's to no avail. The moment my eyes close, I wake up. I think I'm having a series of small panic attacks where I feel like I can't breathe. I feel like I'm drowning and swallowing water. Somehow, I manage to get some sleep. And, before I know it, I'm woken up at 19h00 so that I can get ready for my trek at 21h00. I go to the bathroom and then get dressed. I put on about five layers of clothing because the temperature drops to minus 17 degrees.

The porter says, "Pole pole." Taryn-lee and I are on our way with a group of other climbers.

Although we have headlamps, it's difficult to navigate the terrain. All we can do is focus on the next step. At minus 17 degrees, our water freezes, so I'm thirsty too.

Before we know it, some of the 23h00 climbers catch up to us. They pass us and go up, up, up, their headlamps dimming and finally disappearing.

The night is dark, and the path is hidden, making me feel frustrated, tired, and anxious. As I strain to find my way, my porter, Jackson, offers a piece of wisdom that illuminates more than just the path beneath my feet.

"Cobus, look down," Jackson instructs, his voice calm and steady against the backdrop of my rising panic. I adjust my headlamp and cast the beam of light downward, where it falls on the rocky terrain just in front of my boots.

He asks, "Can you see your next step?"

"Yes," I reply, noticing how the small circle of light made the immediate ground clear and navigable.

"That's all you have to focus on," he says. "Just take your next step. That's all. Just keep doing that."

This simple advice resonates deeply, realigning my approach not just at that moment but also in broader aspects of my life. Though achieving the ultimate goal may seem overwhelming, it can be broken down into small, manageable steps. By focusing on one step at a time, I can make consistent progress, reduce anxiety, and keep moving forward even when things are uncertain or difficult. This lesson from Jackson, illuminated by my headlamp on a dark mountain path, became a guiding principle, reminding me to tackle challenges one step at a time.

Andrea and the rest of our group catch up to us. Some go on ahead, and some stay with us.

At around 02h00, we hear an almighty crash. Andrea fell asleep while walking and then collapsed abruptly.

The porters wake her up and decide that this is a good time to take a break. They give us some hot ginger tea; our saving grace.

I am amazed at how tough the porters are. We're all dressed up for minus 17-degree weather. The porters have maybe one or two layers of clothing. I saw a porter rubbing a woman's hands with his to warm her up. The porters, in my opinion, are the unsung heroes of Mount Kilimanjaro.

I'm so grateful for them for putting their lives on the line for us so that we can have this once-in-a-lifetime experience.

I'm battling to breathe. The team decides to push forward without me.

Jackson and Mufasa stay with me and help me along. With sunrise approaching, we arrive at Gilman's Point, two hours away from our goal, Uhuru Peak.

I see Taryn-lee sitting down. She'd had a tough time of it. She almost fell off the mountain and was saved by one of the porters. As I pass her, we just look at each other, too tired to even greet. I can tell by her demeanour that her race is run.

She didn't have the energy to get to our next stop, which was Stella Point, let alone summit Uhuru Peak. My heart broke for her. And it swelled with pride for her for coming so far. We are still good friends today, and she is one of the bravest people I have ever met.

I was starting to struggle too. I had the first symptoms of altitude sickness, but I didn't know it yet. I sit for a while at Gilman's Point and watch the highest sunrise in Africa.

It was one of the most beautiful sights I've ever seen in my life. I just stared in awe of its greatness. God's creation. Will sits down. He says he'll wait with me.

After a while, I tell him to catch up with the rest of the team and summit Uhuru Peak.

Years later, Will told me that he really wanted to go down because of his asthma. He was struggling to breathe. I also know that he came to check up on me. And, to make sure that I was alive and not dying on the mountain. A guy like Will is tough and was sent on my path for a reason.

Months later, Will told me that he only suggested we go down together because he was worried that I wouldn't go down alone.

That day, at Gilman's Point, Will gave his love to me. I tell him to go and climb that mountain for us. He stands up and makes eye contact with me. He gives me a heart-to-heart hug. We breathe in a little bit and then cough. And before he leaves, he looks me in the eye, and he says, "Cobus, remember why you came to climb this mountain." Then he turns around and leaves. I wanted to climb this mountain for many reasons, including my kids, for inspiration, to have a story to share.

My last reason was to die on this mountain. I shared it with my team every night. And every night they said, "Cobus, you're not going to die. You're going to come back with us." And I said, "No. I don't want to go back."

Almost an hour later, Jackson asks me if I'm going down or if I am going to push forward. I thought, I'm so close, let's go for it.

As the sun came up, the snow started to melt. Walking has become perilous due to the slippery conditions. I kept on slipping and sliding and could go over the edge at any minute. It freaked me out.

I just speak to myself, "Keep pushing. Keep pushing. Don't slip."

Finally, Jackson and I arrive at Stella Point, a whopping 5 756 m up.

I didn't know it at the time, but my race was run. The altitude sickness hit me hard. I wasn't going to be able to summit Uhuru peak.

What Is Altitude Sickness?

Sometimes called 'mountain sickness,' altitude sickness is a group of symptoms that can strike if you walk or climb to a higher elevation, or altitude, too quickly.

What Causes Altitude Sickness?

The pressure of the air that surrounds you is called barometric or atmospheric pressure. When you go to higher altitudes, this pressure drops, and there is less oxygen available.

If you live in a place that's located at a moderately high altitude, you get used to the air pressure. But if you travel to a place at a higher altitude than you're used to, your body will need time to adjust to the change in pressure.

Any time you go above 8,000 feet, you can be at risk for altitude sickness.

Types of Mountain Sickness

There are three levels of altitude sickness:

Acute Mountain Sickness (AMS) is the mildest form, and it's very common. The symptoms can feel like a hangover: dizziness, headache, muscle aches, and nausea.

High-Altitude Pulmonary Edema (HAPE) is a build-up of fluid in the lungs that can be very dangerous and even life-threatening. This is the most common cause of death from altitude sickness.

High-Altitude Cerebral Edema (HACE) is the most severe form of altitude sickness and happens when there's fluid in the brain. It, too, is life-threatening, and you need to seek medical attention right away.

I was in terrible shape. Going to Uhuru Peak would take me two hours, and then I'd have to come back, which was another two hours. It was better to go down to base camp and then to the next camp; an eight-hour walk.

I was so close. I said I'd summit Uhuru Peak and didn't. I was deeply disappointed and, for a while, felt like a failure. Over time, I realised that there were many healthy people that didn't make it either, and some of them never got as far as Stella Point. I'd done it with haemophilia and crutches. That was something worthwhile, wasn't it?

On Day 5, we were all challenged. The wall was difficult; impossible for some. The greatest feat was the immense support every person showed for those in need. It's difficult to give of yourself when you are at a deficit, but solidarity still prevailed.

Limits were pushed far beyond anyone's expectations as emotions ran high. The encouragement to move at a steady pace saved a lot more physical and metal energy than anyone had bargained for.

Though exhausted in more ways than we could count, an air of gratitude constantly lingered around every one of us.

On the mountain, I was really lost in my own thoughts, really, and I asked God, show me. Show me what I need to see. And as if on cue, I felt a guide come up beside me, even though I was alone. I felt like I wasn't just walking anymore; I was being led. That's when I realised, no matter how solitary this journey might feel, I'm not doing it alone. That's been the beauty of this entire trek—not just the physical climb, but the spiritual journey as well.

It's funny how the mountain pulls things out of you. You start off thinking you're here to conquer a physical challenge, but soon you realise it's so much more than that. It's about conquering your inner doubts, your fears, and sometimes your past. Every step up that wall, every breathless moment—it's a step away from who I was and a step towards who I am becoming. It's not just a mountain; it's a metamorphosis.

Will Butler: *And, about tomorrow—yes, we're summiting. But in a way, we've been summiting every day we've woken up here. Every morning that we've faced the cold, the altitude, and the aches but pushed forward anyway, that's a summit in itself. Tomorrow is just a physical manifestation of every internal victory we've had along the way.*

I think we should carry that into tomorrow night. Not just the anticipation of reaching the peak, but the celebration of every small peak we've conquered along the way—every personal breakthrough, every moment of teamwork, every time we chose to keep going when it would have been easier to turn back.

So, as we prepare for the final ascent, let's not just focus on the hardship. Let's remember why we're here. We're here because we chose to challenge ourselves, to grow, and to be part of something greater than our individual selves. We're here to prove that we can face the steep climbs in life and reach the top, not just despite the difficulties, but because of them.

With that spirit, no matter what tomorrow holds, we'll summit. We'll do it together, as a team, as a family. Because that's what we've become—a family forged on the slopes of Mount Kilimanjaro, under the stars, and in the face of the wind. And that's the real victory. That's the real summit.

We all tackled that, didn't we? With a bit of fear, with a bit of exhilaration. That's the thing about this climb: it pushes you to confront your fears, to really face them head-on. And that's how you grow, isn't it? By stepping into the unknown, into the uncomfortable.

I remember standing there for a moment, looking down at the sheer drop, and my heart was pounding out of my chest. But then I looked ahead, where you all were waiting, cheering each other on, and something in me just clicked. It was like, "I can do this. We can do this together." And when I made that step, that leap, it was terrifying and electrifying all at once.

You know, coming here, I thought I knew what challenges looked like. But this mountain, this journey with all of you—it's redefined that for me. Every step up Barranco Wall, every breathless moment, they were more than just physical challenges—they were moments of truth, tests of will, and I feel like I've come out stronger.

And it's not just about conquering a physical mountain. It's about overcoming the mountains within us—the doubts and fears that hold us back. Today, looking at all of you pushing through your limits, it's inspired me. It's shown me that there's no peak too high when you have the right people by your side.

As we prepare for the summit, I'm not just thinking about the climb. I'm thinking about every laugh we've shared and every down-turn we've faced together. These moments have built a bond between us that's as solid as the ground beneath our feet.

So, as we look to the summit, let's not just aim to conquer it. Let's embrace every step, every breath, and every challenge as a part of this incredible journey we're on together. Because that's what this is—a journey. A journey of friendship, of courage, and of discovery about ourselves and each other.

And when we reach the summit, it won't just be a physical place we're standing on. It'll be a testament to what we've overcome and to the strength we've found in ourselves and each other. It'll be a celebration of every step we've taken together, no matter how shaky or uncertain.

So, here's to us, to our journey, to the mountains we've climbed and the ones we're yet to conquer. We've got this, not just because we're strong alone, but because we're unstoppable together. Let's keep moving forward, keep supporting each other, and let's see this adventure through to the breath-taking end.

It's about setting an example. It's not just what we tell others; it's what they see us doing and how they see us living our lives. If they see us confronting our fears, pushing through hardships, and embracing life with positivity and resilience, then they will learn to do the same.

Our actions, our choices—they're not just for us; they ripple out. They influence not just our immediate circle but potentially generations. That's why these moments, these challenges we face and overcome, are so powerful. They're teaching moments not just for ourselves but for those watching, learning from us.

And here, on this mountain, with each step we take, we're embodying the lessons we hope to pass on. The courage to face the seemingly insurmountable, the strength to keep going when it's tough, the grace to accept help when we need it, and the humility to offer it when others do. This journey, it's a microcosm of life's larger journey.

So as we prepare for what comes next, for reaching the summit and the descent back to everyday life, let's hold onto the lessons we've learned here. Let's continue to support each other, to inspire each other, and to push each other to greater heights. Because if there's one thing this mountain has taught us, it's that together, we are unstoppable.

Because I was suffering from altitude sickness, the journey down became a real challenge, and my wish to die almost manifested itself.

I AM HERE FOR A PURPOSE, AND THAT PURPOSE IS TO GROW INTO A MOUNTAIN, NOT TO SHRINK TO A GRAIN OF SAND. HENCEFORTH, WILL I APPLY ALL MY EFFORTS TO BECOME THE HIGHEST MOUNTAIN OF ALL, AND I WILL STRAIN MY POTENTIAL UNTIL IT CRIES FOR MERCY.

When I went down, my potential cried out for mercy, but my mantra resounded. My calves cramped when I went up because I had to climb on my toes. Downhill, my knees took a beating, and my calf cramps were worse. And, of course, my ankles were not doing any better.

It's slippery. I take two steps and then rest for five minutes. I feel like I can't continue. I can't breathe. I start aiming for a rock in front of me, or a bigger rock, so that I can rest. I almost pass out because I can't breathe. Jackson is encouraging me every step of the way. Eventually, I'm so spent that I beg Jackson to leave me to die.

"God, where are you? Have you forsaken me? Please come and take me." Jackson, of course, will have none of it and cajoles, pleads, and motivates me to go down.

In my delirium, I remember two things:

The first is the smell of faeces and the rubbish lying everywhere. The extent of pollution during the climbing season is truly overwhelming. With 30 000–50 000 people ascending Mount Kilimanjaro every year, I suppose it's understandable.

The second thing that horrifies me are the tiny pathways. When we traversed them at night, we didn't realise that we were one step away from death. In the light of day, this became blindingly apparent. How an average of 3–10 people die on Mount Kilimanjaro every year is beyond me. Based on the pathways alone, I would have thought more people would die. The fact that more people don't die is a testament to the skill and dedication of the amazing porters and guides.

The porters started getting worried about me. I'm taking too long. I'm moving. I'm resting more and more. And I'm struggling to breathe. They take an oxygen reading, and I'm in the low 60s. Just to put that in perspective, 95% to 100% is normal. Anything under 88% requires urgent medical attention. There's no doubt that I'm busy dying. I'm going to get my wish, and I'm at peace with it.

By now, the porters are beyond worried. We need more porters to carry me down, as I weigh 120 kilogrammes. They give me marijuana to smoke, as it will open my lungs more so that I can breathe a bit better.

Maybe I should have done the two-hour altitude acclimatisation hike on Day 2, then I wouldn't be in this situation.

I feel myself slipping away. It's time. I'm getting my wish. Take me home, God.

Apparently, God would have none of it.

Our guides manage to get a stretcher up with more porters. They gently place me on the stretcher and start carrying me down. The lower we go, the more my breathing improves. They ask me if I can walk. I get off the stretcher and give it a go. I'm breathing easier, and I start walking.

But I'm taking a lot of strain. When I hear that it is another four- to five-hour hike to the next camp, I almost give up. I grit my teeth and keep on pushing. People are looking at me. I'm on my crutches. I can't breathe. Help me, please. I lean on everything I can. I don't sit down when I rest because it takes too much energy to get up, so I stand, leaning on my crutches. Take two steps forward, and then take a rest. Take two steps forward, then take a break. Finally, the porters can use a stretcher with one wheel, called the Mount Kilimanjaro Taxi. Imagine a wheelbarrow made out of canvas, and you'll get the picture.

Will is there to help, and I'm strapped into a sleeping bag on the stretcher so that I don't fall out on the precarious journey down.

It's a bumpy ride, and I know I've hurt myself. But that's ok because the lower I go, the easier I breathe. I have hope that I may live. We arrive at base camp, and I manage to crawl into my tent and lie down. The rest of our team arrives and checks in on me.

Will is really worried and asks me if I need the helicopter. I say that we should wait and see how I feel in the morning.

I know that Taryn-lee is also struggling, and my heart goes out to her. We managed to sit around the fire and share our day's experience. Well, that was the plan, anyway. The atmosphere was filled with silence and exhaustion. I didn't eat because I wasn't hungry. Some folks were just sitting and eating slowly.

Right there, in my tent, I felt like I was dying. I drifted in and out of sleep that night, and people drifted in and out of my tent to check up on me. When dawn arrived, I wasn't feeling great, and my oxygen levels were still very low.

They're going to organise a helicopter for me. Luckily, my insurance will cover it. Unfortunately, Taryn-lee's insurance wouldn't cover a helicopter trip because her condition wasn't deemed serious enough. She'd have to pay R20 000 to get a seat on a helicopter. Taryn-lee is spent and crying her eyes out. I feel so sorry for her and so helpless that I cannot help her get on the helicopter.

As I board, I feel like such a failure. I can't help Taryn-lee. She has to walk down. I did not reach the summit of Uhuru Peak. And I didn't even have the grace to die.

I spent eight hours in the hospital. I'm starting to feel half human again. There's going to be a ceremony held to celebrate all the climbers. I insist on being there. I'm so happy to see my teammates—Taryn-lee in particular. I don't know how she got down. I really don't know.

She faced the biggest challenge of her life and came through it, ready to celebrate beside everybody else. She never once gave up, and she was an inspiration to us all. Today, she's still an inspiration to me and to the many people that come to hear her speak. At the ceremony, we all got certificates. I got one for reaching Stella Point, Taryn-lee got one for reaching Gilman's Point, and the rest got certificates for reaching Uhuru Peak.

We were so grateful to our guides and porters. Without Jackson and the others, I certainly wouldn't have made it back, that's for sure. Our team left its shoes, socks, clothes, jackets, and tips for the porters. They have so little, yet give so much. I owed them my life. God had sent me angels in the form of these porters.

It was on that mountain that I reconnected with God. Mount Kilimanjaro became more than just a physical challenge; it was a pilgrimage to meet with God. And on that mountain, I reached a turning point. I was reborn. This divine intervention gave me a clear and powerful reason to continue living. My focus shifted towards building a legacy that inspires and empowers others. He called me to heal and deliver people from their pain and suffering and to provide them with hope and unconditional love. My new 'why' was a mission to never give up, and like Elijah, He sent his golden chariot to pick me up. To take me to heaven. He came to pick me up. With the helicopter, my golden chariot.

Before I end this chapter, I'd like to pay tribute to Jackson, my porter, my angel, who stayed with me throughout my Mount Kilimanjaro climb.

He was my motivator and my confidant. He helped carry my bag and crutches when I could no longer go on. He made sure that I had enough to drink and eat every day. He helped carry me down the mountain. He held me. He supported me. He gave me the strength to keep moving forward when every step felt impossible. I will always be grateful for his kindness and selflessness during that challenging time.

Jackson was an angel sent by God. If it weren't for Jackson, there's no way that I would have made it there or here.

Jackson, your humble spirit and big heart will always inspire me to be a better human. You are an angel amongst humans, and I'll always be grateful to have met you.

Taryn-lee Kearney is a top professional speaker and facilitator, taking her BOOMChakalaka brand and infectious enthusiasm across the globe. She has spoken at TedX and is a finalist for the 2024 Woman of Stature. She also received the Stef du Plessis Founder's Award, the highest honour from the Professional Speakers Association of Southern Africa, in 2024.

Chantal Kading still lives in Cape Town. She has impacted 1 million children in the Western Cape through a mindset training programme with WCED. She is also running her recruitment business, Peopleshop, and has created a peak performance programme.

Jason van Schalkwyk is living his dream in Qatar. He runs a successful company called Scuffle Holdings that is focused on bringing combat sports brands to the African market.

Will Butler and Caz Mamotte have a son together but have sadly parted ways. Will has since grown his company, TonTrac, a weighbridge software and monitoring operation, by 300%.

Tanya du Toit stopped coaching to focus on being a full-time homemaker and mother, guiding her children to be their best selves.

Andrea Bogner is a born-again Christian who is actively involved in the church, happily married, and runs her own businesses, Bogner Motor City Workshop and MyKhaya Air B&B.

Returning from Mount Kilimanjaro, I found myself grappling with the realities of daily life. The contrast between the mountain's profound isolation and the bustling pace of society was stark, and reintegration proved to be a complex process.

The experience of having faced and overcome such a monumental challenge had a surreal quality to it; it was difficult to believe I had done it and that I was back in a world that had continued to move forward in my absence.

This transitional phase was marked by its own set of challenges and missteps. For instance, in my excitement and perhaps overzealous state, I announced on a Facebook Live session plans for another Mount Kilimanjaro climb in 2019, which ultimately did not materialise. Such moments remind me of the need to ground my aspirations in reality and the importance of planning and preparation.

Amidst these adjustments, I harboured a deep desire to write a book about my experiences. However, starting proved to be difficult, as life seemed to have other plans. My business suddenly took off in unexpected and exciting directions. I found myself travelling extensively—first to New Zealand to work with Robin Banks, then to Hungary and Slovakia for business, and finally to Las Vegas to celebrate the wedding of my friends, Istvan and Kathrin.

Each of these experiences brought its own lessons and rewards, contributing to a period of intense personal and professional growth. Yet they also delayed my plans to write, keeping me engaged with the immediate demands of my thriving business and personal commitments.

This whirlwind of activity was exhilarating, but it also underscored the importance of finding balance and carving out time for reflection and personal projects, like my book, which remained a goal waiting to be realised.

In 2019, my business reached new heights, expanding rapidly to include a team of eight employees. With this growth, my story evolved beyond just firewalking to encompass a broader narrative of success and influence. As my professional life flourished, I continued to travel extensively, feeding my passion for new experiences and personal challenges.

Amidst this whirlwind of activity, I seized an opportunity to undertake the 5-day hike to Mafadi, South Africa's highest peak (3 446 m), situated in the central Drakensberg mountains.

This adventure was particularly memorable because I was joined by notable figures: Rob Bentele, the winner of 'Survivor,' and Nicole Capper, the runner-up survivor, as well as Mrs. South Africa 2018. Given the stature of the mountain and the fame of my companions, I initially thought the trek would be straightforward. However, this assumption proved to be a mistake.

Despite the excitement and allure of the challenge, I was not adequately prepared for the rigours of Mafadi. The climb was tougher than anticipated, and my lack of preparation became glaringly evident as we ascended. The experience, while filled with valuable lessons about humility and the need for thorough preparation, came at a cost. My body took a significant beating, reminding me forcefully that overconfidence can sometimes lead to an underestimation of real challenges.

Though the journey was physically taxing and revealed my lack of preparation, it also reinforced the importance of respecting nature's challenges and the necessity of physical and mental preparation for such endeavours. With each step up, Mafadi taught me more about my limits and how to approach future challenges with greater respect and readiness.

Reflecting on my experiences, one of the most vital lessons I've learned is about the significance of the company we keep. I've experienced being taken advantage of in my network, where people would promise mutual benefits but disappear once they got what they wanted. For example, someone would involve me in their events, but once their situation improved, they'd vanish until they needed something again. This lack of boundaries left me feeling exploited and hurt, valued only for what I could offer in that moment.

Another scenario involved individuals using my reputation to propel their marketing, promising collaboration but rarely delivering. One person even integrated me into their campaigns, benefiting from my audience, only to cut off communication afterward, leaving me feeling deceived and undervalued.

In certain initiatives, promises of collaboration often turn into one-sided ventures. Despite investing time and resources, organisers neglected their commitments once they used my network. This left me shouldering the burden of success without receiving support or acknowledgment.

People often sought my innovative ideas over coffee, turning casual chats into coaching sessions without compensation.

What hurt most was trusting individuals with payment plans for my retreats, only to be left with unpaid fees while they lived comfortably. I felt worthless, and it raised a light to my tendency to trust too easily, always leading to emotional and financial strain.

It's essential to be discerning about who we allow into our inner circle. The people closest to us can and will shape our lives, influence our decisions, and alter our paths. They can uplift us, or they can lead us astray.

My father often warned me not to be naive, advice that has echoed in my mind through various moments in my life, especially those where I felt used. There were times when I believed in the goodwill of those around me, only to discover that their intentions were not as pure as I had thought. I realised this often too late, notably when these individuals disappeared from my life once their need for me had been fulfilled. This harsh reality taught me that not everyone who is friendly has your best interests at heart.

Being cautious about whom you trust and allow into your life is not about being cynical; it's about protecting your energy and your heart. It's about making sure that those you count as friends or confidants are there for the right reasons and that their influence contributes positively to your growth and happiness—and vice versa. The people in your inner circle should be those who support, encourage, and challenge you in healthy ways, not those who seek to use you for their own ends.

Therefore, it's crucial to take time to evaluate relationships and to choose to surround yourself with individuals who are honest, reliable, and supportive. And to be the same for them.

In doing so, you not only safeguard your own well-being but also ensure that your journey through life is accompanied by those who truly wish to see you succeed.

Before the world was gripped by the Covid-19 pandemic, 2020 began as a year filled with incredible opportunities and milestones for my career. One of the most significant achievements came when Brian Walsh, a renowned figure on the speaking circuit, invited me to be a speaker at his prestigious REAL Success events. This opportunity allowed me to address an audience of 3 500 people in attendance and another 3 000 online, marking a major breakthrough in my professional life.

During this event, I also had the chance to facilitate a unique glass walk experience, where we set up 12 glass walk stations with a dedicated team of 30 volunteers assisting participants as they walked over broken glass. The event was not only successful but also provided me with amazing footage and an exhilarating experience that was a dream come true.

Just a few weeks later, another door opened with Brian: the chance to lead a firewalk for 500 people. 2020 was shaping up to be my biggest year yet, filled with back-to-back breakthroughs.

However, as the pandemic unfolded, it brought unprecedented challenges and put a significant dent in my plans. Events were cancelled, and public gatherings were halted, drastically changing the landscape of public speaking and live training.

Despite these obstacles, Brian Walsh presented another incredible opportunity—this time to participate in his first online summit. In this way, I was able to speak to an audience of 10 000 people, adapting my approach to suit the virtual format. This experience pivoted my career; I began focusing on online summits and started selling other people's products to sustain my income during the pandemic.

Another unexpected blessing came when Chantal Kading, recognising my experience and the impact I could make, involved me in the WCED's Change Mindset programme. This initiative was aimed at training teachers to foster a transformative educational environment, even amidst the pandemic.

Despite the challenges posed by Covid-19, we were contracted to conduct in-person training sessions for teachers, ultimately impacting an astounding 35 000 educators across the Western Cape.

From 2020 to 2021, I took almost 120 flights to the Western Cape, where I trained over 4 000 teachers. This extensive effort was designed not just to enhance teachers' skills but to exponentially impact the lives of millions of children through improved education.

I consider these experiences a gift from God, perfectly timed to support me through personal and global difficulties and to broaden my influence in ways that I never thought possible. Even in uncertain times, these opportunities reminded me that purpose and growth can still happen, despite obstacles.

In 2021, I suffered from a severe case of Covid-19. The experience was daunting and tested my resilience in ways I had never anticipated. Fighting the virus was an uphill battle. Apart from the physical toll it took on me, I also had to face its impact on my mental and emotional wellbeing. Moreover, navigating through its consequences, encompassing my health, work, and ability to support others, made the situation even more difficult to cope with.

However, I came out victorious. Covid-19 made me value life and overall vitality more. It also strengthened my dedication to making a significant difference in the lives of others with my job.

In 2022, as I neared my 40th birthday, I decided it was time to make a big change in my personal and professional brand.

This transformed my brand into 'The Viking,' representing my strength, resilience, and adventurous spirit. This rebranding was not just about changing my professional image but also about embracing a new chapter of life that resonated with my core values and visions for the future.

To mark the significance of this change and to celebrate my 40th, I planned a big reveal at my birthday party, an event attended by 150 people. It was an evening filled with nostalgia and music, a perfect fusion of my past and the journey ahead. I dusted off my bass guitar, an instrument I had not played in years, and started practicing vigorously. The aim was to not only rekindle my love for music but also to share this passion with friends, family, and colleagues.

At the party, accompanied by my friends Brad, Mike, and Isaac, we jammed to classics from the 80s—iconic tracks by U2, Nickelback, and Bruce Springsteen. The music brought back memories and created new ones, perfectly encapsulating the essence of the evening. It was more than just a performance; it was a declaration of my ongoing evolution and a celebration of life's milestones. This musical interlude not only entertained but also symbolised my multifaceted identity—blending the intensity of my Viking persona with the rhythmic harmony of my musical side. It was a night that truly marked the beginning of a new era for me as The Viking, set against the backdrop of beloved tunes and surrounded by the people who meant the most to me.

I lost my way in 2023. It was a pivotal year for me, marked by a rolling barrel of change. It was the year I met a woman who seemed like the embodiment of my dreams—a beautiful dentist whom I likened to a princess. Our connection was deep and immediate, sparking a whirlwind of emotions and experiences. I thought that I'd finally found my soulmate.

However, this relationship, while filled with moments of joy and moments of love, also became a receptacle for personal growth. She challenged me in ways I hadn't anticipated, pushing me to confront aspects of my ego and deeper insecurities I'd long laid to rest. Through our interactions, she tested my patience, beliefs, and flexibility, ultimately teaching me invaluable lessons about myself and my relationships with others.

I am immensely grateful for the time we spent together and the impact she had on my life. Although our relationship did not last, the breakup was the springboard for the next level of my journey. It brought me back to a fundamental connection with my faith, renewing my bond with God and realigning my spirit with what truly matters. This realignment with my spiritual path was further confirmed by three prophecies that came to me during this period, each echoing the divine guidance at work in my life.

These experiences have reinvigorated my purpose and resolve. I am now more prepared than ever to embrace whatever challenges come my way, fortified by the lessons learned and the growth experienced in 2023. I step forward with a renewed commitment to my path, ready to do whatever it takes to fulfil my potential and honour the plans that God has laid out for me.

The year 2023 brought its share of trials, notably a significant downturn in my business—the first of its kind in a decade. Despite the challenges and uncertainties this brought, it was also a year marked by profound demonstrations of faith and resilience. In a time when the logical expectation might have been anxiety and hardship, I witnessed something extraordinary: God's provision.

Even as business opportunities dwindled, my needs and those of my family were met in unexpected ways. This experience deepened my understanding of faith; it wasn't just about enduring the hard times but witnessing the often surprising ways support can manifest. Whether through the generosity of friends, unexpected financial opportunities, or the simple reduction of daily expenses, I saw evidence of a higher plan at work.

This year of scarcity was evidence of the truth that when one door closes, another opens, often in the most unexpected places. It has taught me to maintain hope and to keep faith in the face of adversity, trusting that I am guided and provided for, not just in times of abundance but perhaps most miraculously, even in scarcity.

The future stretches out before me like a blank canvas, ripe with potential and awaiting the strokes of new adventures and endeavours. As I close one chapter with this book, I'm poised to begin another, armed with a rejuvenated brand, a dynamic team, and a clear vision for what lies ahead.

With the partnership of Isaac Gwala, whose talents and perspectives complement my own, we aim to take the world by storm. Our combined strengths in diversity and music, underpinned by our warrior spirits, are the foundation upon which we plan to build our global influence. Together, we envision a future where our collaborative efforts lead to substantial, positive impacts across continents.

My personal dreams extend far beyond the immediate horizons. I aspire to touch over a billion lives, spreading messages of empowerment, resilience, and transformation. The adventures I plan to undertake—climbing Machu Picchu, walking the Camino de Santiago, driving from Germany to South Africa, and traversing from the northernmost reaches of North America to the southern tips of South America—aren't just travel goals; they are missions infused with purpose.

Each journey is an opportunity to connect, learn, and inspire, bringing back stories and insights that can ignite change and foster global harmony.

Moreover, I aim to influence world leaders and global communities towards peace, love, and hope. By embodying these values and sharing them through every platform available to me, whether speaking engagements, music, or simply the way I live my life, I hope to contribute to a world where understanding and compassion transcend borders and conflicts.

The future may still need to be written, but the themes are clear, and the commitment is unwavering. With a heart full of dreams and a spirit ready to tackle the challenges and joys that await, I am excited to see where this journey will take me and how many lives we can touch together. The path is laid out, the vision is clear, and the world awaits.

Notes and Letters from Friends

WILL BUTLER

To Cobus Visser,

The last FIT (Firewalking Instructor Training) retreat I attended was in 2021. On the 108th night, I gained clarity on what I wanted in life. As I sit here today, I have accomplished all of those goals, including completing a triathlon just two weeks ago and winning a white-collar boxing match three months ago.

This was my second FIT retreat with you, Cobus. The reason I attended was the immense inspiration you provided. I stopped chasing approval and the need for a woman in my life. Then, the Universe, God, literally placed someone directly in my path, answering my first ask. I also stopped chasing customers and trying to control everything in my business. The Universe brought the right customers to me. When I attended that FIT retreat, my business turnover was R25 million. This year, it's R100 million.

At that FIT retreat, I stood in the fire for three minutes with you there by my side. I left knowing that if I could do that, I could accomplish anything.

The reason I could stand in fire for three minutes was because you showed me it was possible. When I attended that FIT retreat, I was 98 kg and unfit. I then dropped to 81 kg. I climbed to Everest Base Camp, higher than Kilimanjaro, and climbed two more mountains in Nepal. I came back and signed up for boxing training, attracting the SA and African Heavyweight Champion to be my trainer. I won my first fight and will win more. I did this because I could stand in fire, and I knew I could accomplish whatever I set my mind to.

But the greatest gift, Cobus, was not even on my list of desires because I didn't conceive it could be possible. My deepest desire was for my son. To see him and love him, and the Universe granted me that opportunity. All of this, Cobus, is because of you and the firewalking experience. It made me believe, and because I believed, whatever my heart desired was given to me.

One of the most powerful experiences in my journey with you, Cobus, was climbing Kilimanjaro together. The climb was gruelling, and there came a moment when you felt you could not go on. I remember you contemplating turning back, and I was ready to go down with you to ensure your safety, fearing for your life on that mountain. In that critical moment, we had a heart-to-heart conversation. I reminded you to remember your 'why'—the purpose and drive that had brought you so far. That moment of connection, the heart-to-heart hug we shared, was transformative. It reignited our resolve, and together, on my way back, I found you reached Stella Point—a shock to think you wouldn't follow me. That experience solidified in my mind that, with the right mindset and support, we can conquer any challenge.

Through all these accomplishments, the one thing that got me through it all was mental strength—something I learned while walking on fire.

WILL BUTLER

RENIER HORNE

I am Dragon Heart, Alchemist, Mentor, Healer. My name is Renier Horne, son of William John Horne, husband to Soné, née Gildenhuys, and father to four children, two on earth, Luke and Aimee Michelle, as well as two in heaven, Michael Ryan and Michelle. I am the pure awesome essence of Godly expression manifested in this physical realm and am thus also known as Mr. Awesome.

You may wonder, "Wow, now that's confidence," or think, "That's a bold statement." But why does he mention his lineage?

The truth is, each and everyone in this lifetime is here for a purpose, not to be diminished into a mere existence but towards greatness, living while still alive. As Marianne Williamson said, "Our deepest fear is not that we are inadequate. Our deepest fear is that we are powerful beyond measure. It is our light, not our darkness, that most frightens us."

My opening statement is the result of the influence my friend, Cobus Visser, had on my journey of self-discovery and empowerment.

Let me explain. I was born with a very rare congenital heart disease named Wolff-Parkinson-White Syndrome. This condition debilitated and ruled my life in every way. After school and a couple of short vocations, I started my own IT company. I also studied theology, went into part-time Christian ministry, and was ordained a minister in 1998. Yet still, I was not living.

During this time period, I was head of worship, and this is when I met Cobus due to our mutual talent as musicians through his brother, who played the drums in our band. The first time I actually met Cobus was during an all-night CANSA walkathon, and we instantly clicked.

We talked about music, worship, and our mutual love of playing bass. The friendship quickly grew into Cobus joining the band and playing at the local 'Kerslig, Vers & Melodie' monthly art offering in town.

One day, Cobus attended a two-day self-discovery course that may have had a great impact on him. We spoke about it, and he persuaded me to also attend the workshop. This single event triggered a butterfly effect in my life that I will be forever grateful to Cobus for. It was in this workshop that I was challenged with the question, "Who are you?"

After a couple of failed attempts, I realised that I was defining myself by my name, my relationships, and my faith, but my true self remained unknown.

This is a topic on its own. Cobus later persuaded me to attend the follow-up self-discovery course and again later to enrol in the full certification to become a Life Coach and Neurolinguistic Practitioner. I was now actively growing into my authentic self and had the training and tools to help others as well.

Then Cobus disappeared.

He came back from overseas as a Firewalk Instructor and immediately wanted me to walk on fire with him. I told him that he was crazy and should stop harassing me. We planned a one-day goal-setting seminar shortly afterwards, and of course Cobus wanted to add a firewalk. Again, I said that he was crazy. Cobus persisted.

I remember standing barefoot in front of a 650°C coal bed, wondering, "What the hell are you doing? No normal thinking person in his right mind would want to deliberately walk over fire! Are you crazy?!" Well, I figured I was not normal, so I gathered a lot of courage and willpower, and while the other attendees were motivated by cheering, I walked! It changed my life forever.

In May 2015, I got internationally certified as a Firewalking Instructor and Empowerment Coach by the Fire Institute of Research and Education and progressed to Executive Firewalking Instructor in June 2022. In 2024, I am currently training for my Master Certification and have since walked more than 1 000 times over fire and have also learned how to stand stationary on hot coals.

When you start the firewalk instructor training and when you graduate, Cobus teaches us when to speak the peace. This is to open your discourse with your lineage to honour those that came before you, that shaped you into the person you are today, as well as to honour your legacy—those who come because of you.

His influence in my life sparked my search for healing from my heart disease. In my case of WPW Syndrome, the 'defect' cannot be repaired with surgery as it is too close to the SA node. The chances of me having to rely on a pacemaker after surgery were too great. In ministry, I learned that everything is already within me that pertains to life and godliness, and in life coaching, I learned that we have the ability to change our destiny. This put me on a journey to search for healing. Driven by my faith and training, I stumbled upon an ancient healing modality named Reiki. It has taught me to let go of anger and worry and to be more grateful, true to myself, and kind to all. It has given me the tools needed to heal myself and others, and consequently, I have seen miracles in my life as well as others', and I have since become a Master Practitioner and Teacher of the system of Reiki.

Although I still physiologically have the WPW Syndrome, I experience none of the symptoms. 'As a man thinketh, so he is,' and a lot of my healing was due to this influence from Cobus.

Cobus and I have shared many moments, songs, workshops, firewalk instructor trainings, and walked on countless fires together. We even co-authored three books in a series titled 'Extraordinary: The Power that is You'. These books include all the lessons we learned together. These are the exact same tools that changed our lives for the better that we carefully selected and compiled into three volumes.

Cobus is passionate about helping people become a better version of themselves, sometimes even sacrificing his own wellbeing just to see his fellow human beings do #whateverittakes to excel into greatness. I have personally witnessed him grow from a bit of a shy musician into the Superman of Africa and then into the Viking Warrior he is today.

I am grateful for his influence in my life and honoured to be his friend.

Aho

Renier Horne is a well-known South African-born Public Figure in the Personal Empowerment and Spiritual Development field who gained prominence for his teachings in Holism and the Mind-Body-Spirit-Connection and is the co-author of the book series 'Extraordinary: The Power that is You'. His writings and teachings explore the incorporation of Science and Beliefs, Advances and Tradition, Exoteric and Esoteric, Allopathic and Traditional Medicine.

How I Became "The Girl Who Walks on Fire, That Can Do Anything."

My story starts when I was at the 'top of my game' in my career and thought I had job security forever as I had been working at the same company for 20 years.

Unfortunately, I severely underestimated the deviousness of some of my colleagues. I promoted a fellow female colleague and never realised just how power-hungry she was. In a nutshell, she used all her female wiles on our largely male line management to get exactly what she wanted—me out of the company.

Looking back today, all I can say is that when power and indiscretion collide, there are always casualties. Within a few months, I went from being the quintessential 'golden girl' of the business to nothing. My line manager, whom I had worked with for years and trusted implicitly, retrenched me, and simultaneously, my personal relationship with my then-partner also broke down. As a result, I suffered a physical and mental collapse.

I found myself disillusioned, rejected, and heartbroken, both personally and professionally. People in my industry were shocked, my family was powerless, and I felt as if there was no hope of ever restoring my life, both personally and professionally.

This is where my story shifted, and to this day, why Cobus decided to contact me, I cannot say. What I can say is that, for some reason, this gentle, brave, guardian angel decided not to let me disintegrate completely.

I remember trying to find new employment, but I had lost my confidence completely. I felt that I was not even capable of being a tea lady or a waitress.

Our journey together began when Cobus invited me to attend a function where he and Robin Banks were holding a team-building session. Being the mom of two teenage daughters, I convinced them to attend the session with me. We arrived while Cobus and his team were setting up wood on a grass lane for a big group of people who were going to do a firewalk.

My girls, who were rather spoiled, plonked themselves down on the lawn and watched me work. I started helping pack the firewood on the lanes for the firewalk. It was a big group, so there were several lanes. Cobus then invited us to partake in the firewalking, but as soon as the work was done, we observed a bit and then left.

Life was hard!

I was unemployed with no support system; finding work seemed impossible!

I felt myself slipping deeper and deeper into misery every day. I felt invisible to the world. My so-called 'friends' also disappeared. I had never asked anyone for anything, but it felt to me like people were fearful that I would ask them for help.

During this time, Cobus checked in on me periodically and then one day invited me to his family's game farm for an event. I wasn't sure what it was about and declined with an excuse. However, Cobus did not give up on me. He extended the invitation for the following weekend and even arranged a lift for me. I had run out of excuses and reluctantly said I would attend the event. I must note that Cobus did not tell me it was not just a weekend event but that it would run over a period of five days. Imagine my surprise!

When we arrived at the farm, I found myself in the middle of a FIT training event. Due to my longstanding good relationship with Cobus and his family, I felt I had no choice but to participate, despite all my fears and insecurities at the time.

The next few days turned out to be life-changing. I recall that I hated it at the time; every day stretched me in every way imaginable.

The team working with Cobus and with our group was phenomenal. Cobus surprised me, inspired me, and humbled me. In short, he gifted me with a lifeline. Cobus showed me some people do care.

During that week, I built fires and walked on fire every day. One of the biggest lessons I learned was that the goal is not to walk on fire, but rather, what is your 'WHY'? So every day I walked on fire with a heart full of gratitude to Cobus and Dewald, my then personal trainer. I walked on fire for my children, and I walked on fire to find work.

In addition to walking on hot coals every day during our sessions, I also learned through other activities to rewire my brain and to conquer some of my worst fears.

I also want to highlight that, most of all, Cobus's kindness towards me saved my life. I was severely suicidal before that week. I had no dreams, goals, or a desire to carry on with my life. I could feel how I was slipping away, with no will to live.

The retreat was challenging for me, and I felt I could not really connect with the other people in the group, primarily because my energy and vibration were so low. In essence, I felt invisible.

My own mind was my worst enemy

During that week, Cobus gradually helped me, and without me realising it, he led me out of the dark abyss in which I found myself. When I left the lodge on the last day of the event, the strangest thing happened. Long-time friends of mine called me and offered me a position. It was as if my prayers had been answered. I felt safe because I knew them. In retrospect, I did not realise what could happen as a result of shifting my energy. That week, and the mental and physical shift that happened inside of me, opened up new opportunities for me. I set a goal in front of everyone at the course, saying that I was going to take part in a bodybuilding competition. I did just that, and a week before my 50th birthday, I won Bikini Fitness for all ages under 1.69 m and 2nd in the category for over 35 at a local competition. My social life also shifted; the way I interacted with men was vastly different, and no longer was I the doormat in my relationships.

Believe me, life still threw me lots of curveballs and still does. But today, I take them in stride. Your attitude definitely determines your altitude. I am no longer fearful of life and its challenges. I learned that when life cuts you, just move your feet until it becomes easier.

Cobus, you will always be my hero. You are selfless and help so many people, including me, with your big heart, and you always give to the fullest, never expecting anything in return.

In closing, my motto will always be:

"A girl who walks on fire can do anything."

I met Cobus a few years ago, when my life had, simply put, run dry. I was at a crossroads; my career had stagnated, and I was shifting from one job to the next, always chasing money.

My personal life was in shambles, I struggled with personal and power relationships at work, I was unfit and unhealthy. I had come back to Johannesburg after a year in Cape Town, where I had ruined my career at the time by being involved in a romantic relationship with a staff member reporting to me.

I met Cobus at the estate on which he lived, having reluctantly agreed to meet with him on the advice of my girlfriend, now wife.

I recall driving to meet with Cobus and being desperately unhappy, directionless, caught in a dead-end job at a small training business, and once again looking for an exit.

When I met with him, I remember thinking that I worked with many life and business coaches and that this meeting would most likely be no different. When we started talking, I tried to pose questions that I thought might be difficult for him to answer. To my surprise, he smiled at me, looked me dead in the eyes, and answered every question I posed with consummate ease. He was the real deal!

I was intrigued; here was a man who clearly had his own challenges, and yet he was humble, kind, compassionate, and willing to listen to my story.

In that conversation (and there have been several since then), we spoke about my goals and the power of positive thinking.

We discussed what I wanted for my life, and yes, he challenged me, but gently so.

Cobus's advice was simple yet life-changing. He asked me to read the book Mind Power by John Kehoe and sent me four PowerPoint slides that would serve as my goal-setting and life management blueprint. The first slide was a slide where I had to use a spider diagram to plot my life across various areas such as finance, business, personal relationships, career, etc. On the second slide, I had to detail why I was not a '10' in each area. The third slide focused on setting three-month goals in each arena and deciding how I was 'getting to a 10.' The fourth slide was a Vision Board where I would paste pictures of what I wanted for my life based on the goals I had set.

I completed the goal-setting and Vision Board exercise, read the book at the same time, and within three months I had a new job, which I really enjoyed, finished my master's degree in business, and achieved several other goals I had set for myself. My whole life changed!

This stock-taking and goal-setting process became something I did on an ongoing basis and still do to this day. My life since then has not been without its challenges. I still struggle with some of the same issues I always did, but the fundamental difference is that I respond differently when those challenges arise. I am focused on acting, not reacting, no matter what I face.

Cobus, you are a person who came into my life at a time when I felt I had no hope, when I felt like I was going to end up in a dead-end career, never finding happiness either professionally or within myself. You helped me find direction, to conquer my fears (the firewalks are a massive part of that), and to enjoy every moment of my life as if it were my last. I will be eternally grateful to you for that.

You are my friend; never forget.

DEON GROENEWALD

Superman and I became friends many years ago through social media. We are both part of the coaching and speaking industry. After being online friends for a long time, we finally met in person.

When I met Cobus in real life, I was struck by his humble, kind, and authentic nature. He is one of those special people who leave a lasting impression on you. He makes you feel like he's just like one of us, despite being admired by many.

We talk often, especially when I need some comforting or inspiring words. Cobus has a way of making every conversation special. He is a great man with many talents, and he always makes me feel important.

I wish there were more people like Cobus in the world. Whether he goes by Superman, Viking, or just friend, to me, he is a rare and precious gem in the sea of humanity.

Cobus Visser is one of the most resilient and incredible individuals I've ever met. Despite the immense challenges he's faced, his resilience and big-hearted nature shine through. Cobus, your love and care for people, even during your own battles, are truly remarkable. Your story of overcoming adversity and pushing through with unwavering belief in something special is inspirational.

When I first met Cobus, I noticed his unique way of connecting with people—always heart-to-heart. He's a big guy, like a teddy bear, with a heart that matches his large frame. Cobus's genuine desire to connect deeply and impact lives authentically makes him a special person. Even though we don't talk often, I always feel a special bond with him and believe in the positive impact he can make.

Cobus's introduction of firewalking and other powerful activities to South Africa has been life-altering. I remember struggling with firewalking due to a past negative experience. I remember struggling a lot with other aspects of my life beyond what I could do. I did firewalks very early on with Emile Ratelband, one of Tony's protégés, and I was fine until I tried to teach someone else how to do it. I then burned myself really badly because I didn't realise how arrogant and naive I was about how it worked. Of course, when you have a negative experience like the ones I know you've had, it makes it scarier to try again. I remember many times you brought me into firewalk environments, and I always resisted walking across the fire because of that memory.

I eventually went to Tony Robbins again and actually did the firewalk there, but I still felt awkward. Then, at one of the events we did together, you caught me off guard and said, "Okay, well, if you're not going to walk across the fire, you're going to jump on glass." And weirdly enough, I felt much more comfortable doing that, as scary as the context was. Your belief in what people are capable of being is so special, and your determination and encouragement helped me overcome my fear. Your dedication to inspiring others through these activities is truly commendable.

In 2020, just before Covid-19 hit, you brought the glasswalk to the REAL Success event, leaving a lasting impact on participants. We couldn't do the firewalk because it was at the Sandton Convention Centre, where it wasn't feasible. Instead, I had never seen anyone set up so much glass in so many rows.

Your team was so determined and organised, setting up row upon row to ensure no one missed out on such a unique opportunity. I was in awe of you, and your efforts impacted so many lives.

You're not just about doing these incredible things for which you're highly trained; your story and who you are are what's inspiring and powerful.

My partner and I went back and forth on whether she was going to walk across the glass. I wanted to, so we ended up doing it together.

Your determination to adapt and create meaningful experiences, even in challenging circumstances, is awe-inspiring. Your commitment to helping others, regardless of your own challenges, speaks volumes about your character.

I think that the world has yet to see the power that you're still going to introduce to so many people. Because I've always looked at speakers, wanting them to exemplify what they teach, we're quite blessed at REAL Success to have achieved that with many of our international speakers. Since the day I met you, you've been a person who epitomises what he teaches, and that is just so special. I'm so proud of what you've managed to achieve with it so far. The world is yet to see all of you.

A poignant memory of you is from 2019, when a team member faced a severe emotional crisis. Despite being in the hospital for a major procedure, you reached out to offer support. This willingness to help, even during your own difficult times, speaks volumes about your selflessness and compassion.

Cobus, you live what you teach. Your authenticity and dedication make you a powerful individual. I'm proud to know you and excited to see the impact your book will have.

Love you, brother.

BRIAN WALSH

Diaan Daniels

Renowned Fashionista & My Wardrobe Designer

I am Diaan Daniels, a Fashion Designer originally hailing from Bloemfontein but based in Johannesburg since 2007. I gained recognition for crafting exquisite attire for local celebrities, particularly in the realms of men's wear and bridal attire. My encounter with Cobus Visser occurred when he approached me to design his Viking-inspired look. From our first conversation, a profound fascination with each other's worlds emerged. We shared stories of our career journeys, the heartaches we endured, and our unwavering determination to pursue our purposes and dreams.

Cobus and I found inspiration in each other, as his personal narrative underscored the resilience needed to evolve and become the best versions of ourselves. Our connection transcended mere fashion and business; it was a meeting orchestrated by the universe, emphasising a purpose to enrich each other's lives. It's truly a remarkable pleasure to connect with someone on such a profound level, realising that our encounter goes beyond chance—it is a fulfilment of life's purpose.

Having experienced one of Cobus's inspiring talks and immersing myself in the individuals within his sphere coincided with a period of significant change in my life. It became apparent that navigating these transitions requires acknowledging that we can't face them alone and fretting about an uncontrollable future is futile. It involves introspection, questioning the decisions we make, and discerning whether they align with our true path.

Cobus's narrative that day served as a poignant reminder to rekindle the self-belief we once possessed as children, nurturing dreams without reservations. It emphasised the importance of trusting that things will unfold as they should, encouraging us to dispel fear, as everything we aspire to achieve lies on the other side of it.

Ross Geldenhuys

Audio Reflection on a Firewalk

Yeah, and then obviously later on that evening we got onto the fire, firewalking. Yeah, we got really psyched up and really keen on it. And the best thing about it is that, from what I remember, there wasn't a single person that didn't do it, from our management to our players to everyone in the squad, the physios, the doctors, even the crazy old doc was in there leading the show.

So, yeah, man. Walking on the fire was awesome—it was cool at the time—but later on in that season, when we had to dig deep after our loss against the Sharks, is probably the one where we needed to turn it around, because we should have won that game.

Anyway, in the last minute, yeah, with Curwin Bosch getting the kick, I still remember it like yesterday. Man, the culture that you initiated with us and that we drove throughout the year—you popping in at our home games and wherever we played in South Africa—was awesome, unreal, you really.

We've got like a, I don't want to say a cult, but a cult going, and the King's Army was pretty special all because of the things that we bought from you or stole from you and carried on growing. If only we had another season or two together, that would have been next level.

I still remember against the Lions when we had just come back from our tour, and we were on a high and we walked on glass. In Johannesburg, and yeah, man, the awesome thing about what you did was you tested us mentally just to get shit done.

You know, don't worry about the outcomes. Everything will be all right.

And yeah, man, we just got into it. And we all bought in. We all did it. And it was a really special year. I don't think many Kings teams can say that they should have beaten the Sharks twice, beat the Waratahs in Sydney, hammered, I think, the Rebels, and beat the Bulls in Loftus. If we had a bit more time, we would have given the Stormers a go too.

But yeah, it was awesome. And the best thing about it is that you keep in contact with most of us or all of us. Because we did have something special that year, and it all started with the name Cobus the Firewalker.

LINDSAY WEYER

TWO-TIME RUGBY WORLD CUP CHAMPION
TECHNICAL ADVISOR

Dear Cobus,

2017 will go down as the best year of my life.

It started with the 2017 Super Rugby, and I cannot thank you and Deon Davids enough for taking us (the team) and me on a journey that will never be forgotten.

The Port Alfred weekend with you and your team was out of this world, Cobus.

It allowed everyone to get together as a group and get into each other's space for a change, because in our day-to-day lives, it's an in-and-out scenario. Work hard to play hard. But we forget that we are people; people have feelings; people want to share things; and people need friends they can count on. We became one.

Staring at each other and sharing personal information with each other was incredible. In a straight way, you get to understand what that individual is about and what's going on in his life, and obviously, he gets to understand you. That was deep for me, as you guided us to understand each other and be there for each other.

A warm, solid hug for longer than 3 seconds gives you the feeling of, "I have your back and I care because I am here for you." You get a sense of relief and warmth.

The steel rod—I remember I was paired with some partners that I didn't really have a relationship with—and this gave us the opportunity to work together and forget about the past and that everything will be good if we work together. That helped a lot.

On the firewalk, the mindset to get out there and walk over the coals was literally taking on the challenge with no fear. It showed me that if you think too much and overthink things, that's when you hesitate and your reactions are slow because the coals should burn me, but if you put your mind to it and walk at a steady pace, you will be perfectly fine. Trust the process.

I enjoyed every minute of these activities with you.

From sharing personal information with each other to being in each other's personal space, to working together in team-building scenarios and individually working within yourself to better yourself, striving for the best, and doing absolutely whatever it takes to make yourself and the team successful.

That brought me to tears a couple of times during the camp because you give so much of yourself to the team that you're a part of. People don't see what you go through at work and outside of work. You work so hard to win and make a difference for an individual. Everyone sees the rugby Lindsay and not Lindsay Weyer, the individual.

Cobus, that's where you and your team came in and showed us how to care, love, and work together and to individually do whatever it takes at work and outside of work.

The number of smiles and happiness we all felt that weekend and every day after that was truly amazing and carried on during the competition. That's why we were so successful and won major games at home and away, and we also achieved massive crowd attendances at our Nelson Mandela Bay Stadium during the Super Rugby competition.

The chant you gave us about 'we feel good and happy' was lifting and grew every day on the squad as it became something to look forward to. Every person put a different spin on it, which was great and intense.

 In my line of work as a Performance Analyst, I tend to do all the research and look at trends of the good stuff we were doing and the negative things, then find solutions. In saying that, I strive to grow individuals so that they can perform at their highest and optimal level, as well as make the team perform. I did everything in my power to not only do my absolute best but strive to always make a difference—Never Die Wondering.

The 'Never Die Wondering' attitude is a mindset of living life with boldness and curiosity. It embodies the spirit of seizing opportunities and pursuing dreams without hesitation. This attitude encourages individuals to embrace challenges, explore new experiences, and push their limits, ensuring that they leave no potential unfulfilled and no dream unexplored. It is about living life to the fullest, taking risks, and not letting fear or doubt prevent you from discovering what could be. This philosophy resonates deeply with my journey, where overcoming physical and mental challenges has been central to my personal and professional growth. Adopting this mindset can refocus your approach to life, driving you towards extraordinary achievements and a sense of fulfilment.

In saying that, the team either wins or does not; that's what you get judged on. Sometimes we forget we are still people, and people need backing, happiness, and enjoyment in their lives to go harder and continue to be positive.

People always ask me how I got to the Springboks. It's simple for me: I do whatever it takes to be successful. I had a goal and went for it. I made big sacrifices, I made my family proud, and I made myself happy with my personal achievements.

I hope to go through the same process with you, Cobus, and your team in the future. Your motivation inspires people to want to be the best and to give their best; this creates a good team culture with a good attitude to life and to do whatever it takes.

Barend Pieterse

Former Assistant Coach of the Kings and Griquas &
Current Emirates Lions forwards and lineout coach

Cobus, I want to share some thoughts and experiences that have meant a great deal to me. Reflecting on our time together, there were so many impactful moments.

For me, one of the most significant experiences was stepping out of my comfort zone during those few days we spent together. Initially, I was apprehensive about leaving my room, but the activities we engaged in were the next step I needed to take. As the season progressed, the importance of those days became evident, especially when we were so close to making the playoffs. If we had won that last game against the Cheetahs, we would have had a strong chance of advancing.

I remember going into this experience with an open mind, not knowing exactly what to expect but trusting in the process. Deon had a plan, and it worked out exceptionally well for us. The memories of walking on fire, bending steel, and walking on glass are unforgettable. These activities weren't just about the physical feats; they were about pushing ourselves beyond our limits and discovering new strengths.

The connections we made during that time were remarkable. I still keep in touch with many of the guys, including Deon and Lionel. Many of them have gone on to achieve great things, including becoming Springboks. The lessons learned and the bonds formed during that period played a crucial role in shaping our approach and mindset for the year.

Those few days together and the entire season were invaluable. The experiences we shared, like walking on glass at

Montecasino and other activities, left a lasting impact. It's a testament to the unique journey we embarked on together, and I can't speak highly enough of it.

From a personal perspective, I want to express my gratitude for the journey we shared and the opportunity to get to know you and your team. It was a once-in-a-lifetime experience, one that I wouldn't trade for anything. Your resilience and determination, despite the setbacks you've faced, are truly inspiring.

I'm excited about your book and all the great things you continue to achieve. Whenever you're in Johannesburg, let's grab a coffee or a beer. It would be wonderful to catch up and see you again.

Thank you, Cobus, for the opportunity to share my thoughts. I hope this message helps and conveys how much our time together meant to me. Wishing you all the best with your book and everything else you undertake.

Dear Cobus,

We first got to know you, Cobus, through an agency that organises team-building events and have never looked back since. Our relationship with you is multifaceted: you are a friend, mentor, and business life coach to us.

One of the most significant experiences was when you invited us to a retreat. We attended with open minds, not knowing what to expect, but it turned out to be unforgettable. It taught us a lot about ourselves and about pushing our own limits, both mentally and emotionally.

Your presence and advice have shaped our personal and professional journeys in numerous ways. You helped Silvio delegate certain tasks to management, leading to the smoother running of the company. You also assisted Francesca in forming a marketing division for the Scribante Group.

From you, we have learned the importance of having a positive approach to life and believing that anything is possible if you put your mind to it. You taught us to write down our goals and to apply ourselves to the best of our abilities. You emphasised finding our purpose in life and striving to be the best version of ourselves, doing #whateverittakes.

We will always remember the correct way to hug a person: eye contact—always. 'I see you.' And always hug heart-to-heart, breathing in together and then exhaling. It's an intense experience but very meaningful.

Our father, Celso Scribante, was also a significant influence. A leader, SA racing champion, and Ironman, he fought stage 4 cancer with immense courage, undergoing chemotherapy for three years while continuing to race his heart out. Our father started working for Scribante Construction in 1964 and never left, taking over from his father.

He was a man of integrity who respected everyone he met. His work and family were his life, and his famous saying, "First is first and second is shit," will never be forgotten.

Thank you, Cobus, for the opportunity to share these thoughts. I hope this helps and conveys how much our time together has meant to us. Wishing you all the best with your book and all your future endeavours.

Best regards,

SILVIO AND FRANCESCA SCRIBANTE

Silvio Scribante, the Managing Director for Scribante Concrete, a part of the family-owned Scribante Group, currently holds the title of SA GT 2023 Champion. His sister, Francesca Scribante, also works within the family business, heading up the marketing division for the Scribante Group.

My name is Kerr Walker, and I am a family man first and foremost and a business leader second. I contacted you when I was looking for something different for a team-building event. I wanted an experience that would be out of the box, something like firewalking that no one would expect.

From the start, you emphasised that team building doesn't have a long-lasting effect unless it is followed up with a structured plan for each individual and engages everyone in the process.

Initially, I was sceptical about what you could do for our company, but as time passed, that perception changed. You became a trusted business adviser and a friend.

We wanted you to create leaders out of a young team with little to no experience in managing people and leading a team within an organisation.

One of the most memorable experiences was when we humbled ourselves and offered to wash each other's feet. This was uncomfortable for many of us, but it brought us closer together. We became a tighter group where conflicts were managed quickly and with an open mind towards resolution. The strategy was built together, and everyone bought into what we needed to do.

Your attitude towards adversaries showed us that anything is possible and that we often limit ourselves by our own beliefs.

Over the years that I have known you, you taught me to break the glass ceiling and set goals that are not easy to achieve. You would always ask 'why,' which felt like I had to justify everything to you. However, this questioning made me clarify our objectives and responsibilities. I wasn't aware that I was micromanaging processes within the organisation until you pointed it out. Allowing people to take ownership of their processes made them embrace them as a part of their DNA.

The most memorable moment with you was the firewalk. Many staff members embraced the challenge fearlessly, but I found myself hesitant when it was my turn. We had a chat about the purpose and desired outcome of the exercise.

We wanted a cohesive team that could face adversity together. As the MD of the company, I had to show my commitment by taking on the challenge first. Walking towards everyone at the end of the row of hot coals, the jubilation and excitement were so intense that even the hardest men had tears in their eyes. I did the first walk for my team and the second for myself. This mind shift kickstarted a three-year journey with you.

When you walk into a room, you make an impression. It might be your Superman bandana, your Viking persona, your infectious smile, or your stance. It could be your height, your freshly cut hair, or your Afrikaans accent when you speak English. Whatever it is, you make a significant impression.

I have heard your story many times, and every time I learn something new, whether it's about your two boys who live with your ex-wife or the clashing in relationships due to your constant travels, there's always something new to learn. What stands out the most is that you are a man of your word, with morals and principles. You are a family man, a dependable man, and someone to call for advice. You are a man's man, a man of character, which is rare in today's society.

I am a better husband, father, friend, business leader, and colleague because of you, Cobus, and for that, I am truly grateful. I don't know how long you can continue doing what you do for individuals and companies, but I wish you all the best in the next chapter of your life.

Best regards,

Kerr Walker

Managing Director of SyncSystems Automation and previous Managing Director of Interroll South Africa.

Dear Cobus,

It is with profound gratitude that I pen this note, reflecting on the five-year voyage we've embarked on together. Your role in my narrative is not just as a guide but as a catalyst for transformation, and your indelible influence on Compliance Hub Consulting's story is nothing short of remarkable.

From our first encounter, your vibrant energy and unwavering belief in our potential were apparent. You saw beyond the immediate horizon, envisaging a journey of growth and mutual trust that has since unfolded beautifully. Your conviction in the path we set forth laid the foundation for a partnership that has been steadfast and evolving.

As a mentor, coach, and confidant, you've steered me through the labyrinth of leadership, fostering a culture of accountability and ambition within my team and me. Your dual approach, coupling friendliness with firm guidance, has ignited a transformative spark, encouraging us to transcend traditional ways of operation and fostering a spirit of collective responsibility.

Your teachings have been pivotal, instilling the significance of clear objectives and the strategy to attain them. You've imparted the essence of tenacity: to dream expansively and to construct a future not anchored in yesterday's triumphs but in the promise of tomorrow's endeavours.

During Compliance Hub's nascent stages, your faith never moved, even as we navigated through tumultuous seas. You were the compass that kept us focused, the architect who streamlined our processes, and the cheerleader who celebrated our milestones. Your resilience became our creed, and your dedication, a benchmark for our own.

Now, as Compliance Hub stands proudly on the global stage, your fingerprints are evident in our success. The international accolades, the unique brand we've cultivated, and the spirited team we've built are testaments to the journey we've travelled together—a journey marked by perseverance, innovation, and shared victories.

Your friendship and steadfast support have been my sanctuary in times of doubt, and your relentless encouragement, my spur in moments of complacency. The question of why I endure your constant drive is met invariably with the same answer— it's your unwavering commitment to our collective best.

As your memoir unfolds its pages to the world, I await with eager anticipation to immerse myself in the narrative that is quintessentially you. Congratulations, Cobus, on this milestone, and may it be a beacon to many more achievements.

With deepest appreciation and respect,

HILTON JOHNSON

P.S. The anticipation to delve into your memoir is palpable, and I am eager to witness how your insights will inspire others as profoundly as they have inspired us.

It was a crisp Thursday evening at the Woodlands Country Club, where I found myself engrossed in my PSASA meeting, an event I had grown to cherish. The air buzzed with contagious energy—being amidst individuals equally zealous about serving others was always invigorating. As fate would have it, I ended up seated next to Cobus Visser, and that evening's discussion centred on the art of branding.

Observing Cobus, engrossed in the speaker's words and furiously jotting notes, struck a chord with me. Few matched my enthusiasm for notetaking, and it was through this shared intensity that our connection sparked. Our conversation flowed effortlessly; a shared passion for empowering and guiding others defined our common ground. Truthfully, I hadn't felt like attending that meeting—I was fatigued and drained. However, Cobus's infectious energy worked its magic, reigniting my enthusiasm for my career.

Our dialogue delved into the realm of branding, where Cobus, with his firewalks and his 'Superman' persona, shared his insights. As I expressed the difficulty in finding my speaking identity, Cobus, like a wellspring of creativity, offered ideas. He coined the phrase 'boomchakalaka vibes' to encapsulate my energy, a revelation that resonated deeply within me. That night, Cobus contributed to my journey; henceforth, I was recognised as the speaker exuding 'boomchakalaka' energy.

Amidst the lessons absorbed that evening—both in business and life—I distilled three cardinal principles that have guided me, and I hope they will inspire you too.

Lesson One: Human Connection

Initiate encounters, foster dialogue, and establish connections. Engage by being genuinely interested in others, listening intently, and seeking common ground. Remember, the focus should predominantly be on them, not you. Embrace an open mind and an engaged presence.

Lesson Two: Seeking Support

Don't hesitate to reach out for assistance. Cobus's insight wouldn't have ignited my inspiration had I not opened up about the things that weighed me down. When facing challenges, seek advice or encouragement from others; a conversation can transform your perspective.

Lesson Three: Take Action

Upon returning home that night, I dove into developing my 'boomchakalaka' brand, swiftly translating ideas into action. Many ponder concepts without taking the crucial step forward. Embrace action—even in failure lies an invaluable lesson. Failure isn't defeat but an opportunity to evolve and refine your approach.

In the culmination of my encounter with Cobus, I've realised the profound impact of genuine human connections on one's journey. Our lives are woven with threads of interactions where ideas flourish and paths become illuminated. Cobus not only infused energy into my professional trajectory but also experienced a reciprocal exchange—I contributed to his world too.

Gratitude thrives in genuine connections. Cobus's passion and encouragement were pinnacle, but it was the mutual enthusiasm and engagement that fuelled our connection. These sparks extend beyond individuals; they possess the potential to ripple out and affect the world in a positive way. By fostering meaningful interactions and embracing each person's uniqueness, we sow seeds of change and unity.

Each conversation is an opportunity to learn, inspire, and collectively move towards a brighter future. So, as I encourage you to forge connections, engage earnestly, and make a difference, I also urge you to cultivate appreciation. Acknowledge the impact of authentic connections and cherish their transformative power, for it's within these connections that we find the momentum to advance ourselves and the world.

Eugene van der Merwe

In the world of entrepreneurship, a journey often unfolds like an epic tale, with heroes, challenges, and unexpected twists. My tale, intertwined with Cobus 'The Viking' Visser, is no different. It's a story of transformation, brotherhood, and the pursuit of dreams, marked by laughter, insights, and a touch of the extraordinary.

Our saga began at a personal development event. That's where I first encountered Cobus, the 'Superman from Africa.' Imagine a man with the presence of a Viking trying to fit into a Superman outfit. It was like watching a bear wrestle into a swimsuit—a sight both hilarious and strangely inspiring. In that moment, I knew Cobus was someone who defied conventions, a man who lived life in bold strokes.

The pivotal chapter in our story unfolded at a 5-day International Business Mastermind in Richards Bay. Picture this: two entrepreneurs, a pretty serene night, and a bottle of KWV 5-year-old brandy. At first, it was just a casual drink, but as the night progressed, so did our conversation.

We discovered shared paths and parallel aspirations. With about ten glasses of brandy down—or perhaps more, as my vision had started to double—Cobus began deconstructing my business approach. It wasn't just one bottle; somehow, a second had snuck onto the table, fuelling our ideas and revelations further. But he wasn't just talking; he was reshaping and reinventing my perspective.

By the light of dawn, I had a revamped business plan, a ground-breaking strategy, a hangover powerful enough to floor a bull, and a bond with Cobus that was unbreakable.

Another remarkable chapter was Cobus's birthday event, a task that truly tested our mettle. He asked me to plan and fill his personal development bash with 250 people. "Sure, three months and R100,000 should do it," I said. Cobus's reply? "You have three weeks, and let's slash the budget by 60%." My heart raced, thoughts swirling—this was classic Cobus, turning the improbable into the achievable.

Under Cobus's guidance, my business, Van Studios, transformed from just a business venture into a beacon of innovation. His influence didn't just stop at business strategies; it extended to fulfilling lifelong dreams. I had always dreamt of owning a Ferrari, the kind I had posters of on my wall as a kid. With Cobus's coaching and a newfound business acumen, that dream shifted from my wall to my driveway—a roaring, gleaming testament to dreams turned reality.

But even the mightiest of heroes have their kryptonite. For Cobus, it wasn't a glowing green stone, but the allure of a lady in high heels and a cocktail dress. It's in those rare moments that 'The Viking' loses his unwavering focus, revealing the man behind the legend.

As our journey continues, each day is a new chapter filled with challenges, victories, and lessons. We've gone from sharing brandy-induced dreams in a cabin to turning those dreams into tangible realities. Cobus isn't just a coach or a business partner; he's a brother in arms on this exhilarating path of entrepreneurship.

In retrospect, our story is more than a series of events. It is proof of the power of connection, the strength found in shared visions, and the extraordinary results of pairing a digital marketing entrepreneur with a coach who embodies the spirit of a Viking.

With every step, we're not just building a business; we're crafting a legacy. And, with Cobus by my side, I'm reminded that in this odyssey of ambition and aspiration, the greatest adventures still lie ahead.

My name is Mike Handcock, Chairman at the Circle of Excellence Group, a global entity with clients across more than 50 countries and a notable presence in personal and professional development since 2006. Our accolades include multiple international awards and the publication of seven international bestsellers.

The journey with Cobus Visser began a decade ago, with a brief encounter at one of our events, and was rekindled with vigour at a Johannesburg Mastermind years later. His contributions were invaluable, embodying the essence of our collective wisdom.

Cobus's transformation from a caped crusader teaching firewalking and glass walking to a figure of profound depth and strength mirrors the evolution of heroes of lore. He outgrew the youthful fantasy of Superman to embody the spirit of a Viking warrior—a leader unfettered by kryptonite or any perceivable weakness.

Despite his ongoing health challenges, Cobus has transcended the limitations that fate bestowed upon him. His journey has not been one of succumbing but rather of transcending—to a Viking whose principles are deeply rooted in spirituality and who seeks not judgement but aid for all.

Cobus's impact on thousands is undeniable, whether through his commanding presence on large stages or his intimate gatherings, where he fosters a 'Viking Pack.' These are men united by shared values, seeking to harness the strength they find in Cobus's leadership to conquer their mental, physical, and spiritual boundaries.

Witnessing Cobus's growth into one who leads not with a sword but with wisdom, who transforms lives in one-on-one sessions or in front of crowds, is a profound joy for both Landi Jack and me.

Memorable moments abound, from strumming guitars on his 40th birthday to intimate Masterminds in Santorini, where Cobus, despite his health regimen, remained energetically present and always fully engaged.

Cobus's experience in Santorini, touched by the sacred beauty of its sunsets, is an expression of the need for exploration and the Viking spirit within us—to discover and be spiritually moved by new horizons.

In closing, I assure you, the reader, that you are in the most capable hands with Cobus. You are embarking on a journey with a man who has conquered Kilimanjaro, defying what seemed impossible due to his ailment. Cobus embodies the spirit of resilience, empowering you to face fears and embrace a life of 'no excuses.'

With this narrative, I hope to have captured the essence of Cobus's spirit.

MIKE HANDCOCK

Dear Cobus,

It feels like only yesterday that our paths first crossed in Johannesburg at that Mastermind event, yet here we are, years later, bound by a journey that has transcended the ordinary.

As I lead the Circle of Excellence, a global consortium dedicated to amplifying the influence of conscious leaders, I can't help but reflect on the serendipity of our encounter and the impact you've had on my life.

From the moment we met, your presence was a catalyst for change. As a gold-tier member of the Circle, your commitment over the past year has been unwavering, but titles barely scratch the surface of your role in my journey. You are a true catalyst for change, and the experiences we've shared have shattered the confines of my perceived limitations.

One of the most vivid memories I have is of walking over embers and shards with you—a journey both literal and metaphorical. These acts of bravery revealed the boundless potential of the human spirit, especially when armed with courage and guided by a leader like you.

My path took an unexpected turn after Covid, leading to a sensory transformation and an involuntary shift towards veganism. Initially, this change bewildered me, but through your insight, it crystallised into a poignant revelation. You helped me see that this alignment with veganism was not random but a prelude to my literary exploration into the spiritual essence of animals. Your gentle reminder illuminated the interconnectedness of our journeys and the souls we seek to understand.

Beyond your teachings, you've introduced me to a renaissance of the humble embrace. Your mission to guide men into nurturing deeper, heartfelt connections through hugging has left an indelible mark on me and many others. The simple power of a genuine hug has dissolved barriers to intimacy and fostered profound connections.

When I speak of you, I think of a man who embodies the indomitable spirit of a Viking. Your dedication to living out values such as heart, perseverance, and honour sets a towering standard for others to aspire to. You weave these threads into the very fabric of your business ethos, creating a legacy of integrity and strength.

Two moments with you stand out vividly in my mind. The first is when you shared the enigmatic guidance of a pigeon, a creature that chose you and symbolised the peace component of your warrior spirit. The second is our journey to Santorini, where, amidst a picturesque sunset, I watched you, the peaceful warrior, contemplate life's next chapter with a resolve that commands respect.

As the drums of life continue to beat and the dance ensues, you stand not merely as a survivor but as a beacon of nobility and courage. Your story resonates with the echoes of ancestral Vikings forging through life's blizzards with unyielding determination.

We celebrate your relentless pursuit of greatness, Cobus, and eagerly anticipate the ripples of prosperity, freedom, and purpose that are sure to amplify your influence on the world.

This is more than a memoir; it is an invitation to witness the power of unwavering courage and the relentless pursuit of personal evolution. Readers, as you join Cobus on this journey, may it ignite within you the flame to embrace your own Circle of Excellence.

With deep respect and admiration,

Landi

I am Hungarian by origin, but I have been living and travelling across Europe. I am responsible for factories as a factory manager, working for big multinationals like Essity and P&G, and leading large organisations. My mission is to wake people up from their routines and help them enjoy what they do. There is a lot of fun in showing them the mirror and helping them reinvent themselves and their organisations.

I came to know Cobus Visser when I wanted to do the FIT after reading the book 'Extreme Spirituality' by Tolly Burkan. Accidentally, the South African FIT was the best from a timing point of view, so I enrolled and paid. The rest is history.

I later learned that Cobus, who hosted us on his farm and provided us with the honeymoon suite, did not get paid by the organisers. Cobus, being the generous guy he is, never complained about that.

Cobus is a friend, brother, coach, and mastermind. He was my best man at our wedding in Las Vegas, took my team in Slovakia through the fire (twice), and we had fun times together in Budapest, Slovakia, Las Vegas, and Balaton.

Cobus makes you feel appreciated and listened to, and he brings the best out of you! He boosted the motivation of my team significantly, helped me navigate through some difficult personal times, and pushed me to actively try to resolve my relationship with my daughter.

In a nutshell, he was always there when I needed him to push me, challenge me, and kick my ass when necessary. His great

Kilimanjaro adventure inspired me to climb Kili a year later with Kathrin. It was by far the best adventure we ever had.

During our climb, we faced a particularly challenging section known as the Barranco Wall, which has an elevation of 600 - 800 meters. We were climbing and wondering how Cobus was able to accomplish this feat. My struggle with stomach issues and breathing continued, albeit a bit softer, but it was always looming in the background. I would never advise anyone to do this without proper acclimatization. It's a strange situation, giving your life totally into the hands of strangers. There is no way to quit, and honestly, struggling for days and days is not a lot of fun.

I told Cobus many times that when climbing the Barranco Wall, I first raised the question: how the hell did he do it? But then, the climb to the summit is even more difficult. I have no clue what drove him up there or how he managed to summit Kili.

With Cobus, we have witnessed many ups and downs, twists and turns. I have known him since 2017, when we first met at Baobab. I still remember arriving in the middle of the night. His teachings and philosophies have significantly influenced my mindset, behaviours, and decisions, both personally and professionally.

Reflecting on our relationship, Cobus has played an essential role in my life. His presence, advice, and actions have shaped and changed the course of my personal and professional journey. He is someone who brings out the best in people and inspires them to reach their full potential.

I wish to share with Cobus and the readers of this memoir that knowing Cobus has been a blessing. His support, friendship, and guidance have made a major impact on my life.

Thank you, Cobus, for everything.

Cobus A. Erasmus (Snr)

I've known Cobus The Viking Visser, aka Cobus Superman Visser, since he was just Cobus Visser, the very good friend of my son, Cobus Ash Erasmus Jnr.

Because he tried to rise above his limitations from a young age, I had great compassion for his situation. So when I was asked in 2010 to present a trauma counselling course in Pretoria for ABBO (Christian Radio Counsellors), "Vissie" was one of my first choices as a speaker because of the way he fought his haemophilia with perseverance.

After my grief book, S.T.U.K.K.E.N.D...Life after a Death Shot, appeared in 2011, Cobus once again helped me to market my book by organising a presentation event for me in his hometown.

To top it all off, in 2013, Cobus hosted his first firewalk trial run at our campsite at Glenharvie. That night I attempted the impossible myself—thanks to Cobus's support and encouragement—by walking over the hot coals unscathed. What a triumph!

Little did we realise to what heights Cobus would still rise (literally and figuratively). A mantra of his that I particularly like is: "Life is like an echo: you get what you give."

Thank you, Cobus.

On one of my vision boards, I have written that I want to write a book. I must say I have no idea how to write a book or where to begin. It has been a while since I wrote this on my vision board, but here I go...

The chapter I wrote for the Kilionpurpose book was Basecamp, and it turned into my own personal full-fledged book. I just haven't cleaned it up yet, nor do I know anything about publishing. However, as soon as I started writing, I couldn't stop.

To raise awareness, for me, means that people have to hear the hard truth about what is happening. We need to be open, raw, and transparent. This short book has a combination of it all: stories, metaphors, inspirational messages, and techniques on how I did it. Maybe some of it can help you.

I just came from Tanzania, climbing the majestic Kilimanjaro, the highest mountain in Africa. It was the hardest and toughest thing I have ever done in my life. We were eight people, all climbing for different purposes and causes; we called it Kilionpurpose. My cause was for abused children and animals because they cannot speak for themselves.

My journey began way before the actual day I set foot on the plane to Tanzania. I said yes to Kilionpurpose not because it was on my bucket list, but because I heard from Cobus Visser (a dear friend of mine, SA top motivational speaker, and Master Firewalker who climbed for Haemophilia) that they were forming a group to climb Kilimanjaro for a purpose. I had always wanted to make a difference and raise awareness for abused children and animals, but I didn't know how until this came my way.

One of my challenges was that I didn't have the funds to do this. I am not used to asking people for money; I have always made it on my own. This forced me to be humble and ask people and companies for contributions to our cause. Ask, and you shall receive, and so I did. And WOW, how it changed my perception. You would think that your closest friends, families, and colleagues would be first in line to help you. Well, I will let you finish this sentence.

Isn't it strange and wonderful that total strangers and companies step up and show up? It definitely changed my perception and outlook on life. This has taught me that it takes all kinds of people to make this beautiful world of ours so beautiful. Accept it and move on; don't dwell on it; and most of all, don't take everything so personally. The word 'no' only means NEXT. Go on to the next opportunity.

I learned it's about pushing through. If you want it bad enough, what are you willing to do to make it happen? Is your WHY big enough? I got two big contributions from companies I never thought would help me. It made me humble again, and I realised God has a hand in this. Thank you. For everyone who helped, your name is forever on the flag. I am grateful. Thank you.

When I climbed my mountain, it taught me to be present. There are no distractions on the mountain. No phones, no luxuries. You have so much time for yourself. There is just water when you get thirsty—no Rooibos Cappuccinos, no quick stops to get an ice-cold cola. You only bring with you the necessities to nourish your body so you can reach your goal. After all, this is what I'm here for.

On the first day after a 10-hour hike, we thought that was extreme. Little did we know that the first day was the easiest. We all sat together and reflected on what happened during the day. We highlighted the good and the bad of what happened during the day. We mentioned the strengths and weaknesses of each other and also realised that we actually completed each other. One person's weakness is another person's strength, and vice   versa.

My goal was to climb Kilimanjaro and reach the top, Uhuru Peak, to raise awareness for abused women and children and for a very personal reason. I had gone through a very difficult time after my dad was murdered a few months before.

We arrived at base camp at around 12h00 in the afternoon. The altitude at Barafu Camp is 4673 m above sea level. The top of Kilimanjaro is Uhuru Peak at 5895 m, which is 5 km away. We had lunch and were advised to get some rest. We would start our attempt to summit Kilimanjaro at midnight. Nelson, one of our guides (we had four), thought it was a good plan to let Cobus and Taryn-lee leave at 22h00 because they were slower. The remaining six of us would leave at 00h00, and we would catch up with them on the mountain. Caz and Will also opted to leave with the 22h00 group because they already felt some of the altitude sickness and wanted to take it steady. Myself, Chantel, Jason, and Tanja would go at midnight. Dinner was at 18h00. We prepared for our summit, got our clothing and gear ready, and double-checked all our nutrition, fluids, and snacks for energy. Thereafter, we went to our tents to rest.

Nelson woke us up at 23h30. I was already up at 22h30. I wanted to take my time getting mentally prepared. We gathered at the dining tent at 23h30 where we had the last of our refreshments. At midnight, we all lined up behind each other. From our camp, it is a very steep way up. Breathing is very hard and difficult. Walking is very strenuous and needs to be done in very small steps with deep breaths in and out. The starting point was already a difficult one. A steep hill up until you get to a big uphill slab of rocks where you have to climb over. Our porters and guides helped us because if you slip and fall, it could be fatal. This alone was very exhausting for me, and I needed a breathing break soon after to bring my heartbeat down. It felt as if my heart was beating out of my chest.

It was pitch black. All I could see was the majestic blanket of stars above me and thousands of little lights going up the mountain. We all had our little headlamps on, looking like small ants marching up the mountain, each one following close behind the other.

As you walk, it gets steeper and steeper until you get to big rocks, then thousands of loose stones, and just gravel. It was like that all the way to the top, except at the top parts, where there was snow and slippery ice.

My mountain buddy, Tanya, and I were mainly in front behind our guide. I remember Alex, one of our guides, vividly. The first couple of metres were tough. I kept saying to myself that it would get better. It was a constant 45-65-degree upward climb. It was so steep that we couldn't walk straight up; we had to walk in zigzags to make it easier between loose gravel and stones.

Not a single step was ever easy. The stone and gravel would slide away under your feet as you took a step, making it even more exhausting. What made it a bit more of a challenge were the temperatures.

That night, we climbed the mountain at -15°C. Those who didn't take precautionary measures with their water supply, which consisted mainly of bladders and water bottles, had those totally freeze up. Mine did. Added to this, it was already so exhausting just to suck the water out of the bladder pipe because, on the mountain, there is no energy to waste.

I had a bladder, a normal steel bottle, and an additional bottle with a bag inside. We tried to insulate the plastic pipes from the bladder so that it wouldn't freeze up, but that didn't work.

My pipe, the bladder, and the steel bottle froze up. This was problematic because my one remaining bottle was soon finished, after which we had to share water with each other, our guides, and the porters.

The mountain made me delusional. It played with my mind. I totally lost track of time and my surroundings. I felt like I had turned into a machine. I only cared about my mountain buddy and followed my guide's instructions; it was survival for me.

My life was in the hands of our guide because he knew the mountain and had done it over 100 times. That was my only world for a while until we summited. I focused only on getting to the top. I would see the top of the mountain and push myself with extreme persuasion to that point, only to find it went further up. This happened numerous times.

I blocked out everything else that was happening around me. I did not know where the rest of my group was, how they were doing, or if they were coping.

I began to forget things; my mind told me to quit probably every 10 minutes, hundreds of times. I did not know whether what I was feeling was real or if my body was faking it just to get off the mountain.

My toes were frozen, and my nose was constantly running, so much so that the salt in my mucus was burning my skin until it was red and raw. My lips were so dry and painful; I remember I kept licking them with my tongue, only to find the cold wind would dry them out instantly.

My lips got so sunburned on the previous days because the UV rays on the mountain were so much more intense. The combination of all of that made my lips burst. It was extremely painful.

My ears were covered up, but still, the ice-cold wind got through to them. It felt like when you are flying on an aeroplane and your ears close up. It felt like that, with the occasional stabbing pain flowing unapologetically through.

It felt like my brain was frozen too. Occasionally, I would bash my head with my hand and shake my head so that blood could flow through it or fix whatever was going wrong.

Nausea came and went. My stomach felt like I had diarrhoea, and the headaches intensified as the altitude increased and the air became thinner.

It's amazing how your mind and body just switch to survival mode. This way of thinking and acting has never happened to me. Never have I put my mind and body under such circumstances that ultimately all that matters is LIFE and to survive. Man, what an amazing switch that is.

Suddenly, things that were important to me before I climbed Kilimanjaro no longer mattered.

I remember every time my mind would let intrusive thoughts in, I would sing O Heer my God, an Afrikaans Christian song. I wanted to meet God and my late dad at the top. I felt so vulnerable; I felt ready to die.

There was nothing more I wanted in my life than to stand next to my dad. I was so sure I would meet him at the top. I was like a rock up the mountain because suddenly I had a purpose. The purpose was to DIE.

Subconsciously, I had prepared for my death before I came to climb. I only realised this after I started writing my story. In my testament, I had prepared everything that had to happen if I died on Kilimanjaro, even where my funeral would be and what song would be played. I was ready to summit, meet my death, and carry on with my existence away from Earth. I had nothing to lose, only sweet death to gain.

OH MY GOD... This stopped me in my tracks when I read what I wrote. I had been dead since my dad passed away; we were inseparable.

I had spent every day of my life with my dad, my best friend, my soulmate. There is something miraculous about putting pen to paper. Do you see how important it is to write things down—your thoughts, your feelings, your hopes, dreams, even your disappointments?

It made me realise how strong my body was.

When I would look up, I would see hundreds of little lights. All human beings, attempting their dreams and goals, all fighting their own minds, fighting for their own dreams to reach the top. What a real-life story! We do this every day, climbing our mountains. Your attitude will determine your altitude. No saying was ever truer.

May it be a physical or a metaphorical mountain, whether it be at work, with your spouse, or in life. We all have this light within us that shines so brightly, showing us the way. I call it intuition, the voice of God. But do you follow it?

Some reached the top, but not everyone did. I heard from our guide that out of a group of about 43, only 25 summited.

I remember passing people on the way up; some were so shocked that their whole bodies would just shake. Some lost the energy in their legs and couldn't move further; some froze up. I did not hear of anyone losing their lives that day, but the mountain is no stranger to taking them.

One of the rules on the mountain is to keep moving. "Pole pole," they would say, which means slowly. If you stand still for more than 5 minutes, you will start to freeze.

Our breaks were very short; even in a few seconds, it felt like my hands and feet were about to freeze. My mountain buddy's hands were frozen, and I remember how she cried from the pain.

Our porter named Jackson was so sweet. He would take Tanya's hands, rub them together, blow hot air onto her hands, and give his gloves to her for additional heat. He would climb further without gloves. He sacrificed so that someone else's journey would be easier. How many of us would do this for another person?

I heard someone say to me, "The mountain does not want us here; he will make it hell for us to reach the top." And so he did! He broke me in so many ways. Today, I respect him for his grace and thank him for his mercy.

I wanted to die; he made me suffer mentally and physically. He let me live. I'm sure the learnings and answers will come back to me. All I know is that a lot happened to me on the mountain. There is a reason why I am still here.

The mountain did not give me what I asked for; he gave me what I needed. This is the same in life as well. LIFE does not give you what you ask for; it gives you what you need. Take the lessons and grow. After all, the only place where you will learn and grow is out of your comfort zone.

The higher I climbed, the tougher it got. There were no paths, only snow, rocks, ice, and gravel. Very slippery and dangerous. How typical this is in real life as well, when you walk the road less travelled. It's lonely, hard, and sometimes confusing, and at times we turn back because it's easier down than up.

At one stage, it felt like our guide also lost the trail because we would make our own way over the snow and ice. I have never felt so lost before. I just told myself: You are almost at the top. I cannot quit now. If I can do this, I can do anything.

I have gained so much respect for myself because of my physical and mental strength. I am stronger than I ever thought I would be. It has shifted my bar of expectations to a totally new height. This is typical in life when you reach your goals. You can never go back to the way it was. It changes you when you reach them.

We must all strive for those moments in life when something happens, and you know life will never be the same again. Those are the moments we must seek.

I have one motto in life: If your dream does not scare you, you are not dreaming big enough. Every day, do something that scares you.

Tanya, at some stage, was walking in front of me. The terrain was so unstable and slippery that she slipped and hit her knee on a stone. I remember her just crying from all the pain, cold, and frustration.

I told her that we were not giving up. Not now.

From there, I led the front, and we just kept on going, climbing over iced peaks and making our own way to the top. This is a simple example of why we cannot do things alone in life. We all need someone who supports us and calls us on our bullshit.

One valuable lesson I have learned was from Jason, my fellow climber, because he expressed human kindness to me on the Barranco Wall. It's a part of the mountain that goes straight down on one side, and the path... well, there is one, and then there isn't. You would need a hand to pull you out on the other side. If you slip, you could fall to your death. I have experienced that.

When a hand reaches out, reach back to grab it, even if you think you don't need it. We are always quick to say, "I'm fine," "No, thank you," "I can do this on my own," but we are not meant to do things alone. Everyone here right now is climbing their own mountain. Stop thinking that you are the only one ever climbing a mountain and that your mountain is unique and your circumstances are unique, because they are not. STOP being a victim on your mountain; grab it by the balls and own it. Take responsibility.

I have decided, and hopefully you will too, to take the hand. It made me feel so cared for, wanted, and safe.

So, by this time, ¾ up the mountain, I just lost all my primly woman behaviour. There were strange noises coming out of my mouth as I pushed through the gravel and heavy ice, which stood out like hundreds of little ice peaks. Almost like Sylvester Stallone noises, with every effort up, I would go, "Aargh, huuuuh," up the mountain. Loudly. Because this is what I was feeling—very expressive.

I remember the sun coming up. Oh my God, how beautiful and relieving it was. These were the signs that we were still alive and not in hell. The sun on my face would warm me up, releasing new energy and faith. I learned here that every day is a new day, and every day comes with its blessings. Every day, we can start fresh with new energy and a new way of thinking.

Our guide told us that we could have a 5-minute break at Stella Point (the second-highest point of the mountain).

We didn't make it to Stella Point to have our ginger tea. We were too exhausted. I think they saw that we needed it NOW. They stopped us all; we gathered, and our bodies signed off relief when the heat from the tea flowed so calmly into our frozen bodies. I wanted to eat a protein bar, but it was impossible; it was frozen solid.

We didn't stay long as it was too cold; better to keep moving.

I can't remember how long it was. All I remember was forcing myself through little ice peaks when a sign caught my eye. Never in my life have I seen something more beautiful than this board. I didn't even know what it meant or what it was. All I knew was that it meant something. Life had given me a sign. Do you see the signs when life gives them to you, or do you just keep on complaining and ignoring them?

I summoned my last bit of energy and will and forced my body forward. Tanya was behind me. I collapsed on a stone under the signboard—STELLA POINT—and just started crying. All the pain, frustration, and pushing myself came out of me.

Afterwards, we laughed about it because we called it UGLY CRYING, and that is exactly what it was: very loud and very unapologetic crying. Chantal, Jason, Caz, and Will joined moments later, expressing the same emotions. Cobus and Taryn-lee were still behind us on the mountain. Never in my life have I heard grownups cry like this.

Our guide informed us that Uhuru was still a few hundred metres away. After going through so much, I never thought it would end. We hugged each other, cried together, calmed each other down, took photos, and prepared ourselves for the final destination.

Again, the mountain did not make it easy for us.

Tanya, our guide, Alex, and I began first. Each of us took our own pace. Now you start walking for yourself and your reason WHY. This is one goal you have to finish on your own.

From Stella Point upwards, there are no more stones and gravel, just snow and ice. It had not been snowing for the past few days. The snow had melted and frozen hard.

Every function in your body is difficult. The feeling of 'I don't care anymore' had set in my body. I remember I had five layers of pants on me and on top as well. Some layers I bought were oversized to make sure I could fit all of them on.

I didn't have the energy to pull my pants up again if they slid down my butt. I didn't care anymore. I just left it.

My jacket, which I opened up with four layers underneath, gets really hot when you start moving. My face was burned red from all the mucus running down. It felt like it was frozen on my face. I started wiping at it with the clothes on my body. I just didn't care what others thought anymore. I bet they did the same.

I was physically exhausted. As I attempted the final destination, I remember dragging and scoffing my feet, taking mini steps. But as I was walking, I fell asleep. Lucky for me, one of my feet started slipping on the ice, and it shocked me awake again.

For a moment, I was gone. I had an angel with me, keeping me on my feet, I swear. This could have been the moment I prepared to die.

From there on, I prayed to God to keep me awake. I repeatedly told myself, "Stay awake, stay awake." This is how exhausted I was and how willing I was to let go of my life. It was so easy to let go at that point.

I had a chance to die. Something let me live; my soul is not done yet.

Tanya and I were the first to reach Uhuru. Strangely, we were not in a celebratory mood. It was incredibly hard. We had enough; we were finished.

It was super seeing our KILICRAZY friends arrive one by one, uniting with us at the top—our dream, our goal, our purpose.

They say that once you reach the top, the view is beautiful. And it is, but it comes at a cost. You will leave a different person than the one you were when you came. Again, I will say it: You will leave a different person than the one you were when you came. That means that when you go back to the place you came from, everything is different, because it's not the world that has changed; it's you that has changed.

It broke my ego—who I thought I was. In time, it will be replaced with the reborn me, the person God kept alive to fulfil my purpose. In some way, I did die on that mountain that day.

We had 31 porters serving us in extraordinary ways. Without them, this would not have been possible. My question to you is: How do you treat the people around you that serve you every day, ensuring you reach your destination?

Yes, I'm talking about the cleaning lady, the guy who puts petrol in your car, the lady who serves you food. Yes, I'm talking to every single person that crosses your path daily and makes your life easier. And yes, I'm even talking about your toothpaste and toilet paper. Even they fulfil a purpose to make your life easier. We have all experienced what it feels like when your hand reaches out to that roll and it's empty.

When last did you say, THANK YOU, THANK YOU, THANK YOU?

There is a saying in life: if you don't appreciate the small things in life, how will you appreciate the big things in life?

I dedicate this climb to my life, my son, and my late father.

Cobus, I wish you all the best on this incredible journey with your book. Thank you for your unwavering friendship and for inspiring me and countless others to reach for our dreams. Your strength and resilience continue to light the way for many. Thank you for being such a pivotal part of my journey.

With heartfelt gratitude,

ANDREA BOGNER

Eulogy

for a Life Lived with Passion and Purpose

To be read at my life celebration.

Ladies and gentlemen, family and friends, as we gather here today, I urge you not to mourn but to celebrate the life that I was so blessed to live. Remember, I am not truly gone; I continue to live within each heart that I've touched and within every life that I've influenced.

Thank you to everyone who has been a part of my journey, teaching me lessons and helping me grow stronger through every challenge and heartbreak. To my family, know that I lived the best life I could, constantly learning and striving to better myself. I leave you with this advice: never give up, follow your dreams, fill your life with memorable moments, and always surround yourself with greatness.

My life was a testament to the power of a second chance. On the slopes of Mount Kilimanjaro, I was reborn. I embraced the purpose God bestowed upon me, dedicating my life to serving Him and touching the lives of others. My mission was to bring hope, share unconditional love, and inspire people to move from darkness to light, to prophesy, and to bring healing to those in need.

Looking back on my life, I can see something beautiful that was created with dedication, resilience, and immense faith. My life was shaped by the lessons taught by my beloved mother, the challenges faced with my brothers, and the unconditional love given by my children.

I implore each of you to live a life filled with purpose. Embrace your challenges as opportunities to grow, and allow your experiences to make you stronger. I try to set a good example as a father, brother, son, and friend to show that even in tough times, it's possible to make a big impact.

I was a man who believed deeply in the power of legacy—the kind of legacy that isn't about wealth or material possessions but about the richness of one's spirit and the love one shares. And so, as I bid you all farewell, remember to love fiercely, act kindly, and walk humbly with your God.

As you leave here today, remember me as someone who lived passionately, loved unconditionally, and believed profoundly in the goodness of life. Carry forward the lessons I've shared and let them light your paths as you continue your own journeys.

#WHATEVERITTAKES

In every challenge I faced, my philosophy was simple but firm: do 'whatever it takes.' This belief was not about recklessness but about a steadfast commitment to achieving goals, regardless of the obstacles. It was about pushing past the expected, reaching beyond the comfort zone, and persisting when others might give up. Whether it was scaling the heights of Mount Kilimanjaro, overcoming health challenges, or leading a business venture, the core was always the same—persevere with purpose and passion. Embrace this ethos in your own lives; let it guide you to accomplish the extraordinary and remember that the journey towards greatness is often paved with persistence and unwavering dedication.

One of the greatest lessons I hope to leave behind is the importance of living life without regrets. Look back over the landscape of your past, not with sorrow but with appreciation for the moments that shaped you. Every decision, every crossroad, and every outcome was an opportunity for growth and learning.

Live boldly, make decisions that align with your heart and soul, and act in ways that reflect your deepest values. Fear not the possibility of making a mistake, for it is through these that we gain our greatest wisdom.

Let your life be led by the desire to never wonder 'what if,' but to always know, 'I did all I could.' Live so that when your final sunset comes, you can say with certainty, "I lived fully and loved deeply." Embrace every moment with courage and intention; lead lives that are not only successful but also significant and fulfilled.

Know that I loved you all deeply and appreciated every moment we shared. You have enriched my life beyond measure, and for that, I am eternally grateful.

A Father's Parting Wisdom

To my beloved sons, remember this above all: I love you, and I am immensely proud of each of you. You are the source of my greatest joy and my proudest achievements. As you continue on your paths, I encourage you to embrace the role of fatherhood with enthusiasm and wisdom. Learn from my journey and the mistakes I've made along the way—I gave you the best of myself within the limits of my knowledge and abilities. Strive to be the great dads that I know you can be, nurturing and guiding your children with love and patience. Remember, I love you 'lots like jelly tots'—a simple, sweet reminder of the boundless, playful love I will always have for you. Go forth with courage and love, and make your mark on the world as wonderful fathers.

A Challenge for a Lifetime

As I leave you with these final words, my challenge to each of you is to embrace the power of connection and compassion in your everyday lives. Share the hug I have taught so many and teach people the hug, spread love, and pay it forward—human connection is a force that binds and heals. Live each day without regrets, as if it might be your last; never shy away from doing whatever it takes to forge the life you dream of. Hold faith in God as your cornerstone and North Star, allowing Him to guide you, focus your path, and enrich your spirit through prayer and meditation.

Imagine your life as a journey through a vast, beautiful forest. Each day, you have the opportunity to gather firewood. This firewood represents the memories, experiences, and lessons you accumulate over the years. As you walk through the forest, some days you find plenty of dry, easy-to-carry wood—these are the joyful moments, the successes, and the love you share with others. Other days, the wood is harder to find or heavier to carry, symbolising the challenges, heartbreaks, and hardships you endure.

But remember, each piece of firewood, whether light or heavy, is essential. Over the period of your life, gather as much firewood as possible. Embrace every experience, cherish every memory, and learn from every lesson. When you are old and sitting next to your fire, it is this firewood that will keep your soul warm. It will be the stories you tell, the wisdom you share, and the love that continues to burn brightly long after the fire has started. So, go and make memories, gather your firewood, and ensure that your fire burns warm and bright until the very end.

I urge you to build a legacy that outlives you, one that can be passed down through generations, filled with stories of courage, love, and faith. Write the book of your life with actions that speak of your heart's passions, your unwavering strength, and your boundless compassion.

Love fiercely, play wholeheartedly, and remember that life, in all its complexity and beauty, moves swiftly like a blink— make every moment count, make it memorable, make it meaningful. This is your story to tell, your life to live, your legacy to leave.

To all gathered here today, let this not be a goodbye but a celebration of a life fully lived and a mission fulfilled. Go forth with the fire I've passed on to you, and let it illuminate your way.

Thank you, and God bless.

I am seeking your support as a fellow believer who holds strong faith. Throughout my challenges, God has consistently provided signs, symbols, and opened doors for me. Now, it is time to live out this faith. Here are the last three prophecies over my life that continue to inspire and motivate me.

As we come to the end of this book, I reflect on what's next for me. I need to be reminded of my calling and purpose. I am sharing the following not only for you but also to remind myself that God has a purpose for my life. I must not give up and must live each day fully.

I ask for your support, to stand in agreement with me, as it is written: when two or three gather in His name, it shall be done on earth as it is in heaven.

Thank you for being part of the next chapter of my life. The past is now laid to rest; it is time to build a new future.

It is not only time for me to rewrite my stars, but for you to rewrite yours as well.

"Do not seek for things to happen the way you want them to; rather, wish that what happens happens the way it happens; then you will be happy."

EPICTETUS

One

Prophet Leon du Preez

The enemy has tried to come in. Even as I'm looking at you, there's a fire going this gentle. So, there's a ministry call—a very strong ministry call—on your life. Stand up for me. Come stand here in front.

Luke and Mark. Okay. So that's significant because those are two names that are together. What's your name, sir?

Cobus, I saw when the Lord said ministry, I see a ministry on your life. There's a great anointing on you for generations before there's an evangelistic anointing in you, and the Lord wants to open your mouth to speak with fire because it will cause your hands to lay upon people and deliver them and set them free from demonic spirits.

But there is pain that has been there for many years of almost abandonment. The Lord is saying I'm going to heal your heart in a great way. And there's a fire that is going to come upon you. Because you are supposed to be holding a microphone and be preaching fire, be preaching miracles, be preaching deliverance.

But an eruption came in somewhere, or a shift came in somewhere, where the enemy tried to lie to you and say who you are not, who is the opposite of exactly who God has called you to be. For the Lord is saying, "I've called you." To pre-prospering and there will be financial blessings, but I saw this ministry and I saw many praying for you, generations before you. It is like a mother or grandmothers or people before you praying for you because there's a word that God is watching over you on the inside of you, not only as an evangelist but even as a prophet because there will be a prophetic word. They'll come out of your mouth under an evangelistic anointing, the mantle of an evangelist, the mantle of fire will be upon you for the Lord is saying I will raise you up.

I'll train you up under my spirits because you've searched, and you've searched long, and there's this hunger that is in you. And you said, I don't want the fake, I don't want it; I want the genuine. If this anointing be genuine tonight, may the touch of God come upon you. May the spirit of God that is real in my life and that has raised me up out of a drug den touch me in a drug den.

Where the power of God came on me in a drug den. May this anointing touch your heart and bring out the gift and the treasure that is in you. For I prophesy tonight, I speak forth tonight, Father, under the oracles of God, by the power of the Holy Spirit, that in three years, there'll be a shift when people look.

Now I speak this word into any form of darkness and even death that tries to come to you. And even death that tried to take you more than once and is planning to take you again. I cancel every contract against your life. I cancel every agreement against your life and every spirit that tries to torment even in the night watchers, to say you're not good enough in this area.

I cancel those words for I speak by the power of the Holy Ghost, for the Lord is saying: *I'll establish you, son, and I'll raise the work around you.* For there are things that didn't want to come to pass because of an agreement in the past. An agreement of many years ago that has allowed for a spirit to come in and try to take a life and to bring death.

But it shall not be so. For I saw death trying to come even in family around. But I cancel this agreement. For the Lord is saying you will live long. And you will live a prosperous life, so do not fear that your life will end soon, for you will live long, and the days of your life will be long, says the Spirit of God.

But the Lord is saying: *Tell him I'll take his heart, and I'll run with him speedily; I'll give him a mantle of fire, and even the microphone that you're holding, he will speak with under a fire and anointing, and we'll use him in a certain part or certain city and cities.* Says the Spirit of the Lord, for my mantle comes upon him this night in Jesus' name.

Rivers of living water out of his life. I pray that authority will be deposited into him tonight. Anoint his hands with healing. Anoint his hands with deliverance. In Jesus mighty name. Give him the anointing. Double that which I have received. May a mantle come on him. I saw him travelling for some reason.

City...in a city and something. It is only by the fire and the unction of the Holy Ghost, touch them tonight, ignite the evangelistic mantle, ignite the evangelistic anointing, and the fire of the Holy Spirit.

Touch this life. Come on, let's give Jesus a praise offering. There's not even a doubt in my mind. I can say that I'll stand before God one day and answer him straight on this. You are called as an evangelist. Called to inspire. Called to be an evangelist, to witness, to have a testimony to share. Like I said, death has come numerous times in the name of Jesus Christ.

What is the connection to Cape Town? Do you have a connection to Cape Town?

Yeah, I just always have a longing to go to Cape Town, but I don't know at the moment what that connection might be.

Okay. No, no, that's fine. So, you stay around here?

I stay in Centurion.

Centurion? Oh, right here. Okay. Okay. I saw a connection to Cape Town, but there's a ministry that God has for you.

For the Lord is saying that I'll protect you and there is an area where I see in front of me standing somebody who is supposed to have millions and will have millions. For you will meet the right person who will open up certain things for you. But be very careful. In the name of Jesus Christ. Amen.

Amen. Awesome.

Two
Prophet Jean-Pierre Bekker

Jesus. For I hear the Spirit of the Lord say that He has seen the hunger of your heart. He has seen the thirst in your heart for more. And know this: God will respond to the desperation of your heart. The Spirit of God has been luring you, and the Spirit of God has been pulling you closer to Him. For it is in this intimacy and in this becoming more acquainted with the resurrection of His power that the Spirit of God will begin to resurrect, revive, refresh, rejuvenate, and restore even that.

Which has been lost through losses. You have to endure but know this by my spirit of my power, even tonight. You will begin to see the restoration of lost years. For even this year there will be an acceleration where you will not even feel like you have missed out on anything. For by the power of my spirit, by the power of my grace, and by the power of my words, I would now cause an anointing to come upon your life. For it is this anointing that will catapult you into the fullness of the power of my glory, in the fullness of what I have called you to manifest in your generation.

For I'm bringing you into the fullness of the expression of my spirit. For this, you will know visions and dreams, for as I will visit you in the night watch and I will, I will visit you, and I will show you the great and mighty things.

For there is the crowning of the Lord and there is the anointing that I see in the spirit to rise and succeed even when it comes to business, for the spirit of God wants you to know that that world shall open up further and that world shall open up wider, for the spirit of God is calling you now up higher, for there shall be an ascension even tonight and there shall be an ascension into an anointing to thrive in the realms of business.

There shall be an anointing that will come upon your life tonight that will remove the limitations and that will catapult you into the place that God has destined you to experience. I see the limitless access that will manifest for you in the marketplace and in the business world, says the spirit of God.

She's alive. Holy Ghost. Touch his life. He's also healing your heart, for the enemy came in when it came to relationships, and there and there and there, I will bring healing to your heart and I will bring restoration in your heart, and I will touch your heart even tonight by the power of my presence, by the power of my glory, by the power of my anointing, says the spirit of the living God. Wherever you go, fires are lit.

A fire. He makes no apology to set things on fire. He is a fire. Fire has a purpose, and that's to set things on fire. You are the fire. You carry the fire. You're burning with fire.

So, the scripture says in Exodus 12 and verse 2, I feel the Holy Ghost here.

THREE

Apostle Wikus van Rooyen

For his life, Lord. When I looked at you tonight, I saw that at the age of 15, 14, 15, there were some tough, difficult relationships in your life. The Lord is going to take you to a place where you're going to have so much revelation in that realm of relationships. Specifically, many fatherly figures, not specifically your father, can be your father, but I saw fatherly figures that let you down as a young man.

I see how you will be an inspiration to many young men around you. Art will elevate you. There is the breaking away of things around you that's gonna set you up for high things, set you up for mighty things, that's gonna take place in your life. Even tonight, I don't know why I keep seeing the age of 15, the age of 15, that there were certain painful things that took place at the age of 15.

The Lord is gonna remove that. I dunno if you've dealt with it. Are you comfortable with it, or they, those painful things that are putting you back to that nature, tell you God is taking it back to the root to elevate you into. Unprecedented success, unprecedented success. Many people's lives will be impacted as the flow of the Holy Spirit comes to flow through your life like never before.

Certain changes, certain things are going to take place, but just hold on to God. Because he will remove everything that he doesn't want there to be, because he knows what he wants to do in your life. As they're coming together, I see it, like two rivers—glory and presence, glory and presence, that will flow through your life like never before.

Inspiration—I see it all around me. Revelation flowing, revelation flowing, revelation, teaching, revelation, teaching, revelation, where you will speak the word and the heavy weight of God's glory will come to impact people around your lives in the mighty name of Jesus. Father, I seal this word tonight, the mighty name of Jesus.

Even as you take him back to the age of 15, you uproot every thought, every pain of past disappointments in the mighty name of Jesus. I pray, Holy Ghost, that you will elevate into a new exposition in your presence and your glory like never before.

Touch, the touch of the master. Jesus, so much.

Cobus Visser is a renowned South African author, speaker, trainer, facilitator, life coach, and firewalking instructor who is dedicated to helping individuals, business leaders, and people with disabilities.

Over the past decade, he has worked with thousands of individuals and local and international leaders, teams, and organisations to achieve peak performance.

Cobus holds a BBA in Marketing Management from the IMM Graduate School and is close to completing his MBA in Marketing at the University of Edinburgh. He is also expertly qualified as a Certified Master Firewalking Instructor, a Certified Master NLP Life Coach and Trainer, an Executive Business Coach, a Peak Performance Coach, and a Shadowmatch and Enneagram facilitator. In addition, he has completed courses in Applied Sports Psychology, Train-the-Trainer, and Mental Strength, among others.

The great-grandson of South Africa's first president, CR Swart, Cobus was born in Vereeniging and matriculated from Hoërskool Piet Potgieter in Potgietersrus, Limpopo. After being diagnosed with haemophilia as a child and enduring excruciating pain for years, he found himself in the hospital, unable to move, in 2013. Instead of giving up, Cobus decided his body would no longer be his prison.

He has since not only learned to move his arms, crawl, and walk, but he has also conquered Mount Kilimanjaro.

It is this lived experience that drives Cobus to motivate and inspire others and to succeed in various professional arenas: he is the only Master Firewalker in Africa; his executive coaching helps driven, powerful, forward-thinking individuals achieve more impact with less effort.

As a global speaker and business strategist, he uses his inspiring life story to help individuals and businesses reach their full potential, and as a team-building facilitator, he uses a variety of activities—from glass and firewalking to board and arrow breaking and hula-hooping—to help teams understand each other better.

Cobus possesses an insatiable appetite for helping others and, despite being in constant pain, for continuously growing and challenging himself. In line with this, the peak performance expert recently introduced his new brand. Previously known as Africa's Superman, his rebranding as Cobus Visser the Viking is in line with his own personal and professional growth in recent years.

He has co-authored three books, Extraordinary You 1, 2, and 3, with the late Renier Horne.

Since starting this journey, Cobus has twice been honoured with the Men of Valour award. He has also achieved several personal and professional milestones, with climbing Mount Kilimanjaro on crutches and speaking in front of 3 500 people on stage and 10 000 people online standing out as highlights.

Cobus lives his life according to two maxims: #whateverittakes and #livewithoutregret, and spends his free time travelling, hiking, watching movies, and broadening his horizons by completing short courses on various topics. Cobus currently lives in Centurion, Gauteng.

Acknowledgments

I am grateful for the many incredible individuals who have supported, guided, and inspired me along the way as I reflect on the journey that led to this book. This book is a tribute to the community that has been by my side through thick and thin.

First and foremost, I want to express my gratitude to God for always holding me through difficult and joyful times.

Theunis and Ansie Visser – My parents, your unconditional love has been my foundation. I am forever grateful.

Mar-nelle Visser – My ex-wife, thank you for teaching me about love, resilience, and forgiveness.

Tiaan and Wihan Visser – My sons, you inspire me every day with your strength and kindness.

Riaan and Pierre Visser – My brothers, thank you for your companionship and encouragement on this wild ride of life.

William Meyer – Thank you for assisting me, being my hands and legs, and being my driver. Your jokes always lightened the mood and kept me going.

Cobus Ash Erasmus – My brother and friend, thank you for always being there, especially during pivotal moments like my first public firewalking event. You are my saving angel.

Hannes Dreyer – My mentor, your wisdom and guidance have been crucial for my personal and professional development.

Charles Horton – My multimillionaire business mentor, thank you for training me in firewalking and helping me to become a master firewalker.

Steve Consalvez – Firewalk master, always ready to give advice like Simon Cowell—true, honest, and loyal. You have been another invaluable mentor.

Eugene Haines – For your friendship over the last three years and sponsoring me to make this book a reality. Thank you for believing in me, my brother from Ireland. Love you.

Deon Davids – World Cup-winning rugby coach, thank you for your support, believing in what I can bring, and trusting me to do what I know is right with your teams.

Will Butler – Your encouragement, especially during our climb up Kilimanjaro, has been invaluable.

Chantal Kading – Like a mother and sister, your care and dedication, especially during our work impacting over 4 000 teachers in the Western Cape, has been extraordinary.

Jason van Schalkwyk – My brother on Kilimanjaro, your energetic spirit and creed of 'whatever it takes' are inspiring.

Andrea Bogner – Ironwoman, we conquered Kilimanjaro together. You are a rock.

Krupa Ratanjee – For your unwavering friendship during the good and bad times, and for being one of the best partners I have ever had. I will always love you, and I am deeply grateful for your presence in my life.

André Ernst of Maluma Avocado, Allesbeste – Thank you for financing my entire 2018 Mount Kilimanjaro trip. Without your help, I may not have made it.

Tanya du Toit – My first ever public firewalk attendee who became a friend and climbed Kilimanjaro with me. Thank you.

Taryn-lee Kearney – My fellow Kilimanjaro climber and top professional speaker, always ready to give advice and brainstorm with me. You are Mrs. Boomchakalaka, always pushing me.

Carrie-Ann Mamotte – For your love and kindness on Kilimanjaro.

Istvan Takacs – My client from Hungary who became a friend, giving me the opportunity to transform a factory in Slovakia for Essity and also including me in your Elvis wedding in Las Vegas.

Giancarlo De Nadai – My Brazilian brother and friend, always ready to be there and give love.

Hilton Johnson – Client and friend for four years from Compliance Hub. Together, we had some good times. Love our breakfasts, and I appreciate your belief in me.

Lionel Cronjé – Fly-half rugby player, for your friendship and your amazing speech and thanks at the end of the season, you are a true champion.

Makazole Mapimpi – World Cup wing, for carrying the 'whatever it takes' spirit with you.

To the rest of the Southern Kings of 2017 and the SWD Eagles from 2015.

Lindsay Weyer – World Cup Springbok tech advisor, thank you for your faith.

Barend Pieterse – Rugby coach, thank you for your belief, warmth, and support.

Jackson of Kilimanjaro – My angel on the mountain, carrying my bags and motivating me.

Diaan Daniels – Sponsor of my suit and clothing, making me look like a million dollars.

Brad– Charles Lansdown Tailored Leather, for making my Viking outfit look fabulous like a true Viking should.

Patricia – House manager, thank you for all the breakfasts and help.

Goodwin – Working hard behind the scenes to make every firewalk perfect and cleaning up, never complaining.

David – RIP. A man who, from the beginning, was the best firewalk assistant, always making sure every firewalk was a perfect experience.

Renier Horne – RIP. My spiritual shaman and prophet. You will surely be missed. Always ready to take my phone call and guide me when I was lost. You co-authored three books with me and were the best friend I could ask for. Thank you.

Isaac Gwala Seroke – Zulu firewalk drummer, meeting you was divine. Together, we will change the world. Just have faith; it is coming. Let's do this, champ.

Scribante Family – I am grateful for your steadfastness and expert advice. GT3 champ Silvio, thank you for your friendship. Like your amazing dad Celso always said, "First is first and second is shit." That will stay with me.

Hannes Jordaan Attorneys – Thank you for your professional guidance during my divorce and for the personal presence and friendship you offered.

Malcolm Moodley and Romy Chanee – You two were there for me when I needed people the most; when I couldn't walk, making sure the firewalks didn't end. I am forever grateful for you.

Dr. Elaine Ellan – You tested me and helped me reconnect with God, my saviour. I will always love you, and I am forever grateful. I will always pray for you. Thank you.

Gerduan Kemp – Thank you so much for taking the time to create such a beautiful cover photo and for the incredible photoshoot. Your talent and effort have truly brought my vision to life, and I am immensely grateful for your contribution.

Sasta Kuppan – Your amazing support and presence have been invaluable in getting this book ready for promotion. You showed up at the perfect time, and your assistance has made all the difference. Thank you for your dedication and hard work.

Jacques de Villiers – Thank you for your invaluable help, guidance, and friendship in getting this book off the ground. Your thoughtful insights and support have been crucial in this journey.

Alishia van Deventer – Thank you to you and your Starburst Promotion team for your patience and for going the extra mile. Your commitment and effort have been instrumental in bringing my Brand to the public. Thank you for amplifying my voice and my message.

Tolly Burkan – Father of Firewalking, forever changing my life. Thank you for the gift of firewalking and creating the FIT certification.

Cobus A. Erasmus (Snr) – I would like to express my sincere thanks to Uncle Cobus Erasmus for his unwavering support, mentorship and encouragement during my journey, as well as for his help in editing my book for the Afrikaans translation. His belief in my potential and his own inspiring example were instrumental in achieving my goals.

To all my students, followers, friends, and everyone else who has influenced me, thank you for enriching my life and work in countless ways.

If I've missed anyone, please know that every act of kindness I've received has left a lasting impression on me and has not been forgotten. This journey would not have been possible without each one of you.

Are you ready to share your unique voice and captivate readers worldwide? Contact us today to learn more about our author-friendly publishing process and bring your books to life.

CONTACT SASTA VIA

INTONENATIONINTERNATIONAL@GMAIL.COM

In-Tone-Nation | THE MEGAPHONE OF THE PEOPLE

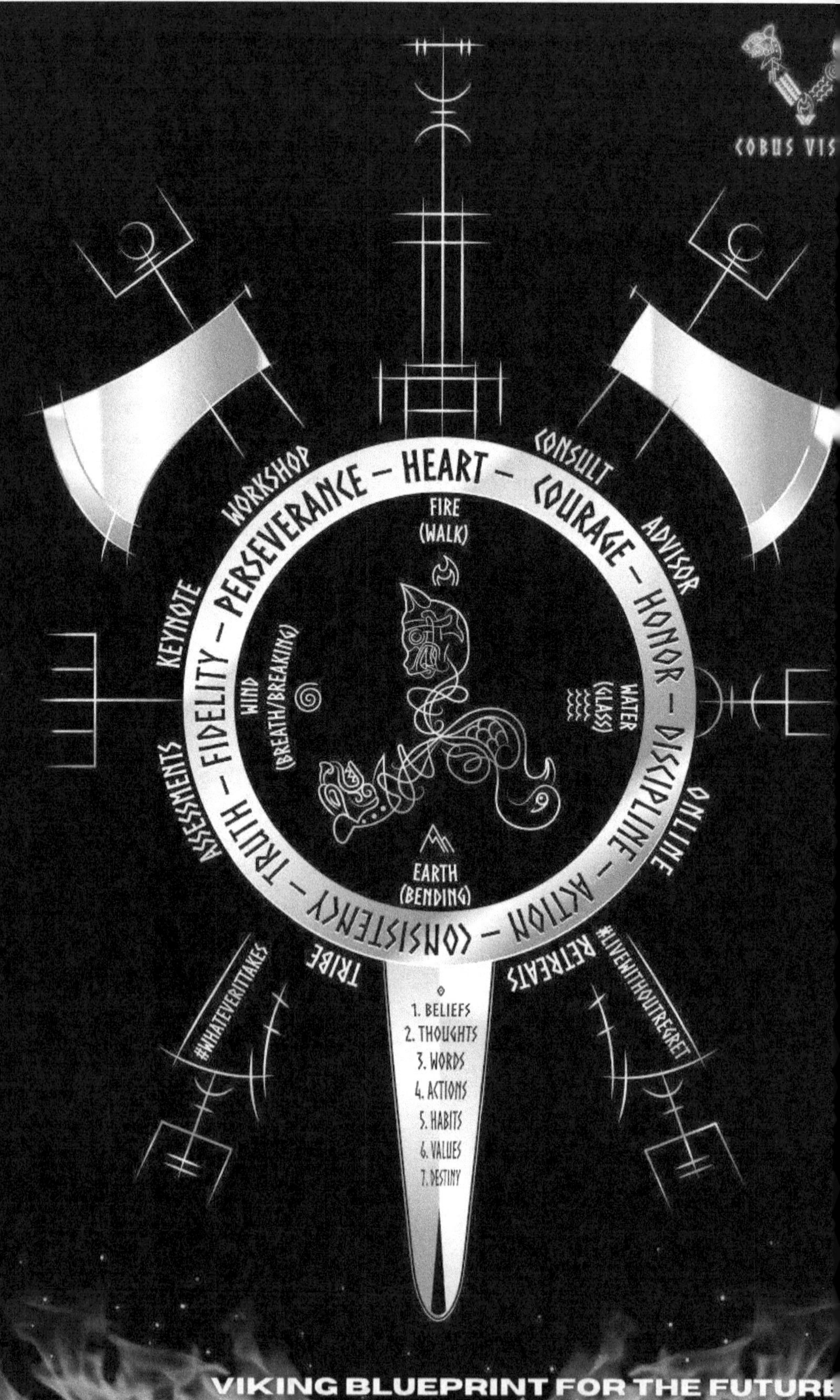
COBUS VIS
WORKSHOP
CONSULT
ADVISOR
KEYNOTE
PERSEVERANCE — HEART —
COURAGE — HONOR —
FIRE
(WALK)
WIND
(BREATH/BREAKING)
WATER
(GLASS)
ASSESSMENTS — FIDELITY —
TRUTH —
CONSISTENCY —
DISCIPLINE —
ONLINE —
ACTION —
EARTH
(BENDING)
TRIBE
RETREATS
#WHATEVERITTAKES
#LIVEWITHOUTREGRET
1. BELIEFS
2. THOUGHTS
3. WORDS
4. ACTIONS
5. HABITS
6. VALUES
7. DESTINY
VIKING BLUEPRINT FOR THE FUTURE

Congratulations
Super Cobra
F.I.R.E.
MASTER
2014
WELCOME
ALL SIZES
ALL COLORS
ALL AGES
ALL CULTURES
ALL SEXES
ALL BELIEFS
ALL RELIGIONS
ALL TYPES
ALL PEOPLE
AND DOGS
SAFE HERE
FAMILY

'DAD, YOU ARE DEAD TO ME

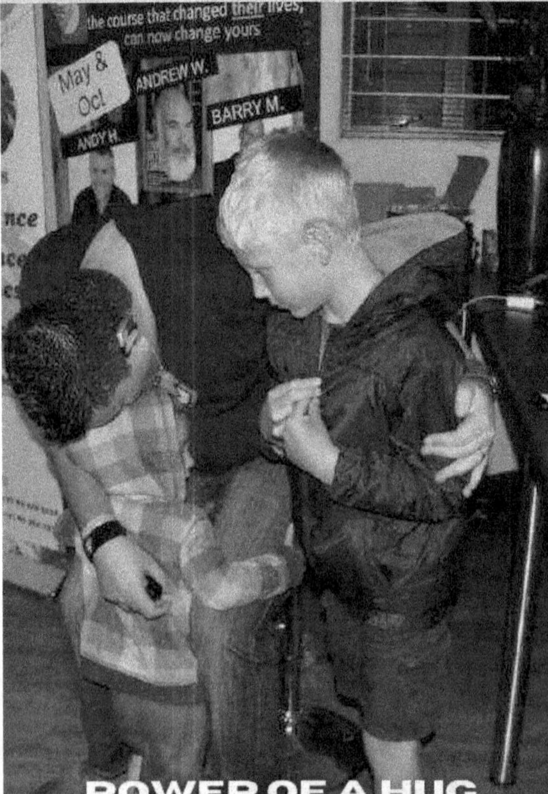
the course that changed their lives,
can now change yours
May & Oct
ANDREW W.
BARRY M.
ANDY H.
POWER OF A HUG

My Dad
DAD
'DAD, YOU ARE ALIV

WHO WANTS KISSES?
2020
TIAAN, WIHAN & DAD
2022

WIHAN WALKING ON GLASS
CR SWART & CORNELIA WILHELMINA
MY GREAT-GRANDPARENTS
CORUS THEUNIS & ANGIE VISSER
FIREWALKING AFRICA
WIHAN

MY GREAT GRANDFATHER
CR SWART
FIRST STATE PRESIDENT OF THE
REPUBLIC OF SOUTH AFRICA

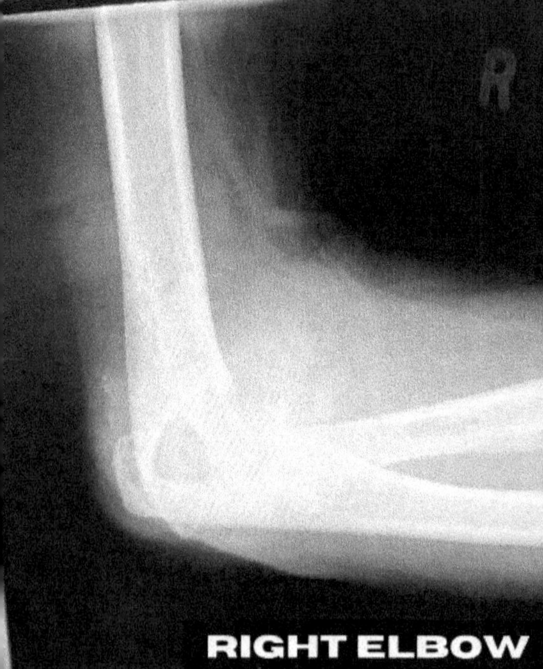
SSER   JACOBUS
/11/1982 Doctor
R
RIGHT ELBOW

BREAKING A BOAR

BREAKING AN ARROW
WITH MY THROAT

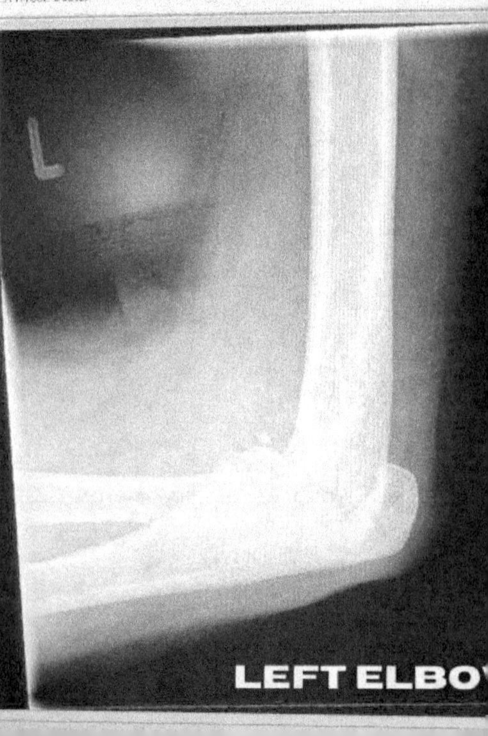
SSER   JACOBUS
2/11/1982 Doctor
L
LEFT ELBO

AS VEGAS WITH ELVIS

OFFICIATING MY YOUNGEST
BROTHER'S WEDDING
RIAAN & COBUS

MY BROTHER PIERRE & I
ROFLIGHT - ENGINE FAILURE

I COULD NEVER PLAY RUGBY
BUT IT BECAME A PART OF ME
NELSON MANDELA BAY STADIUM

Talullah
EARTHSTONES & Samadhi
010 600 0376
DAVID, KRUPA & COBUS
OUR TRILOG
RENIER HORN
REST IN PEAC
Extraordinary
The power that is You
Volume 3
Cobus Visser & Renier Horne
Extraordinary
the power that is you
Volume 2
Cobus Visser & Reni
xtraordinary
ie power that is you
Volume 1
us Visser & Renier Horne

LIVE IN FRONT OF 3 500
SANDTON - A DREAM COME TRUE
CONFERENCE INTERVIEW BY SUSANNA
3 500 ATTENDEES
Cobus Visse

ME & THE KINGS
WWW.COBUSVISSER.COM
SOUTHERN KINGS
Southern Kings
Super Rugby 2017
Campaign 6wins

SWD EAGLES RUGBY
www.swdeagles.co.za
HERO
SWD EAGLES RUGBY TEAM 2015
WENT ON TO WIN 6 GAMES IN A ROW
A DREAM COME TRUE
SWD TEAM BEFORE THE FINAL GAME

WHATEVER
IT TAKES
2
WHATEVER IT TAKES
ON A KINGS JERSEY 2017
MAKAZOLE MAPIMI
WHATEVERITTAKES 20
DEON DAVIDS
& COBUS
#whateverittakes
2017 THE KING
RUNNING OUT TO PLA

DINNER - DAY ZERO
TEAM KILIMANJARO 2018

PLASMA INJECTIONS
DAY 1 KILIMANJARO
QUOTE BY OG MANDINO ON MY HEART
& BRUISES FROM MY CRUTCH

BARAFU CAMP

DAY 2 ON KILIMANJARO

MOUNT KILIMANJARO
CONGRATULATIONS
YOU ARE NOW AT
STELLA POINT
TANZANIA
STELLA POINT

TANZAN
BARAFU
ELEVATION: 467
TATION ZONE:
ROM BARAFU
STELLA POINT:
URU PEAK:

THE PORTERS
MY ANGELS

COBUS & JACKSON

KILIMANJARO NATIONAL PARK
TANZANIA

HIGH CAMP
ELEVATION: 3950M a.m.s.l
VEGETATION ZONE: WOODLAND

FROM HIGH CAMP TO-
BARRANGA CAMP: 3KM (1.5HRS)
CAMP: 4KM (3HRS)
8.3KM (7HRS)
9KM (10HRS)

JACKSON CARRIED ME & MY BAG
ON KILIMANJARO

THE MOMENT WITH WILL
WHEN I WAS GIVING UP

BEING LOADED ONTO THE KILI TAX

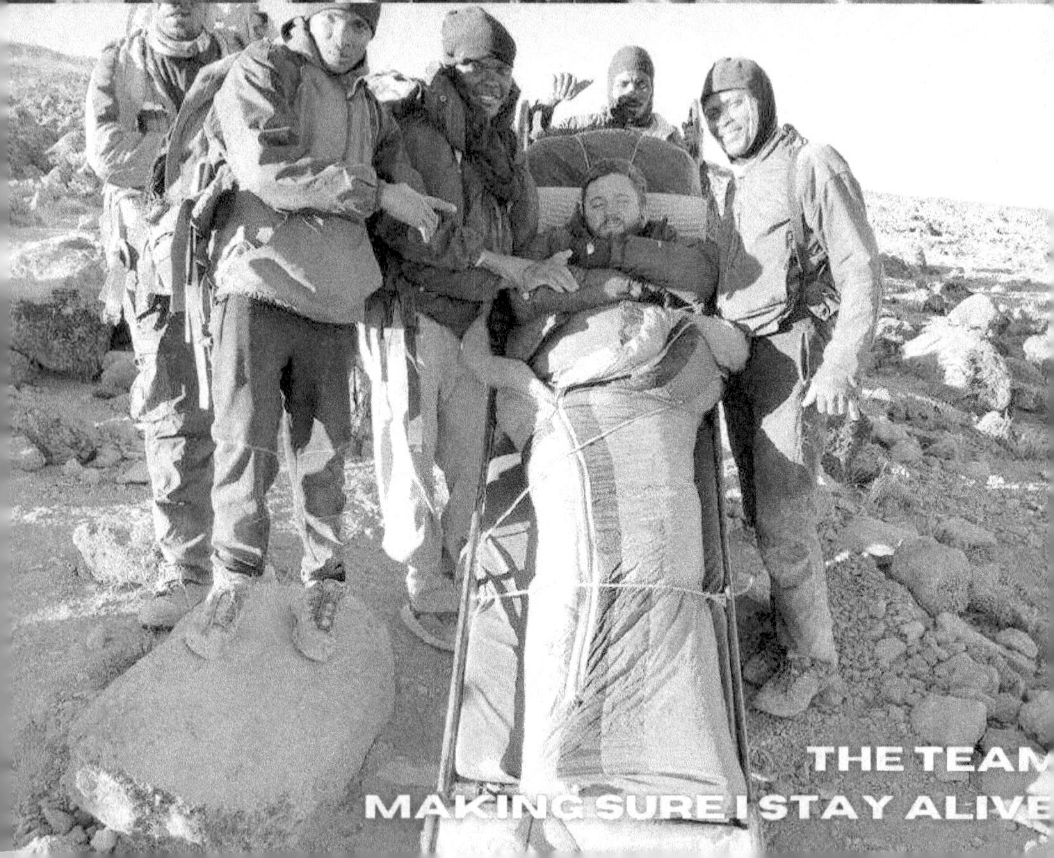

THE TEAM
MAKING SURE I STAY ALIVE

MALUMA AVOCADOS
ZANDER ERNST & COBUS
HIS FATHER - ANDRÉ ERNST
SPONSORED MAKING
KILIMANJARO A REALITY
SURVIVED KILIMANJARO
INSTRUCTOR
MENTOR
CHARLES HORTON

THE BEST PART OF KILIMANJAR
YOU ARE IN HEAVEN LOOKING DOW
ON THE CLOUD

VIKING ICE PLUNGE
EUGENE VAN DER MERWE
& WILLIAM MEYER
LOVE WHAT I DO
FIREWALK RETREAT

SHAPING YOUR DESTINY
WITH ROBIN BANKS

ROBIN BANKS & COBUS

JEANNETTE INTRODUCED ME TO THE
HISTORY OF VIKING SPIRITUALITY

JOHAN MY SWEDISH VIKING BROTHER

ISAAC AND THE VIKING

EUGENE HAINES & COBUS IN IRELAND
MY GOOD FRIEND & SPONSOR
MAKING THIS BOOK A REALITY
MY FIRST VISIT TO IRELAND
EUGENE & COBUS

WWW.COBUSVISSER.COM
WWW.COBUSVISSER.COM
WWW.COBUSVISSER.COM
COBUS VISSER
COURAGE - FREEDOM - LE
#WHATEVERITTAKE
#WHATEVERITTAKES
WILLIAM & GODWIN
MY TEAM
3 500 PEOPLE WALK ON GLASS

DREAM COME TRUE
IN FRONT OF 3 500 LIVE AND 3 000 ONLINE
FIRST SYD ROBIN BANKS EVENT 
IN CRUTCHES

1ST FIREWALK
COBUS ERASMUS
& MENTOR HANNES DREYER
2011

COBUS VISSER

THE VIKING IS BORN

IN VIKING HONOUR - FIDELITY - HEART